Contents

F

F

Use of guidance

THE APPROVED DOCUMENTS

This document is one of a series that has been approved and issued by the Secretary of State for the purpose of providing practical guidance with respect to the requirements of Schedule 1 to and Regulation 7 of the Building Regulations 2000 for England and Wales.

At the back of this document is a list of all the documents that have been approved and issued by the Secretary of State for this purpose.

Approved Documents are intended to provide guidance for some of the more common building situations. However, there may well be alternative ways of achieving compliance with the requirements. Thus there is no obligation to adopt any particular solution contained in an Approved Document if you prefer to meet the relevant requirement in some other way.

Other requirements

The guidance contained in an Approved Document relates only to the particular requirements of the Regulations which the document addresses. The building work will also have to comply with the requirements of any other relevant paragraphs in Schedule 1 to the Regulations.

There are Approved Documents which give guidance on each of the parts of Schedule 1 and on Regulation 7.

LIMITATION ON REQUIREMENTS

In accordance with Regulation 8, the requirements in Parts A to D, F to K and N (except for paragraphs H2 and J6) of Schedule 1 to the Building Regulations do not require anything to be done except for the purpose of securing reasonable standards of health and safety for persons in or about buildings (and any others who may be affected by buildings or matters connected with buildings). This is one of the categories of purpose for which Building Regulations may be made.

Paragraphs H2 and J6 are excluded from Regulation 8 because they deal directly with prevention of the contamination of water. Parts E and M (which deal, respectively, with resistance to the passage of sound, and access to and use of buildings) are excluded from Regulation 8 because they address the welfare and convenience of building users. Part L is excluded from Regulation 8 because it addresses the conservation of fuel and power. All these matters are amongst the purposes, other than health and safety that may be addressed by Building Regulations.

MATERIALS AND WORKMANSHIP

Any building work which is subject to the requirements imposed by Schedule 1 to the Building Regulations should, in accordance with Regulation 7, be carried out with proper materials and in a workmanlike manner.

You may show that you have complied with Regulation 7 in a number of ways. These include the appropriate use of a product bearing CE marking in accordance with the Construction Products Directive (89/106/EEC)[1], the Low Voltage Directive (73/23/EEC and amendment 93/68 EEC)[2] and the EMC Directive (89/336/ EEC)[3] as amended by the CE Marking Directive (93/68/EEC)[4] or a product complying with an appropriate technical specification (as defined in those Directives), a British Standard, or an alternative national technical specification of any state which is a contracting party to the European Economic Area which, in use, is equivalent, or a product covered by a national or European certificate issued by a European Technical Approval issuing body, and the conditions of use are in accordance with the terms of the certificate. You will find further guidance in the Approved Document supporting Regulation 7 on materials and workmanship.

Independent certification schemes

There are many UK product certification schemes. Such schemes certify compliance with the requirements of a recognised document which is appropriate to the purpose for which the material is to be used. Materials which are not so certified may still conform to a relevant standard.

Many certification bodies which approve such schemes are accredited by UKAS.

Technical specifications

Building Regulations are made for specific purposes: health and safety, energy conservation and the welfare and convenience of disabled people. Standards and technical approvals are relevant guidance to the extent that they relate to these considerations. However, they may also address other aspects of performance such as serviceability, or aspects which although they relate to health and safety are not covered by the Regulations.

---

[1]   As implemented by the Construction Products Regulations 1991 (SI 1991/1620).

[2]   As implemented by the Electrical Equipment (Safety Regulations 1994 (SI 1992 No. 2372)).

[3]   As implemented by the Electromagnetic Compatibility Regulations 1992 (SI 1992 No. 2372).

[4]   As implemented by the Construction Products (Amendment) Regulations 1994 (SI 1994 No. 3051) and the Electromagnetic Compatibility (Amendment) Regulations 1994 (SI 1994 No. 3080).

When an Approved Document makes reference to a named standard, the relevant version of the standard is the one listed at the end of the publication. However, if this version has been revised or updated by the issuing standards body, the new version may be used as a source of guidance provided it continues to address the relevant requirements of the Regulations.

The appropriate use of a product which complies with a European Technical Approval as defined in the Construction Products Directive will meet the relevant requirements.

The Office intends to issue periodic amendments to its Approved Documents to reflect emerging harmonised European Standards. Where a national standard is to be replaced by a harmonised European Standard, there will be a co-existence period during which either standard may be referred to. At the end of the co-existence period the national standard will be withdrawn.

THE WORKPLACE (HEALTH, SAFETY AND WELFARE) REGULATIONS 1992

The Workplace (Health, Safety and Welfare) Regulations 1992 as amended by The Health and Safety (Miscellaneous Amendments) Regulations 2002 (SI 2002/2174) contain some requirements which affect building design. The main requirements are now covered by the Building Regulations, but for further information see: *Workplace health, safety and welfare: Workplace (Health, Safety and Welfare) Regulations 1992, Approved Code of Practice*, L24, HMSO, 1992 (ISBN 0 71760 413 6).

The Workplace (Health, Safety and Welfare) Regulations 1992 apply to the common parts of flats and similar buildings if people such as cleaners and caretakers are employed to work in these common parts. Where the requirements of the Building Regulations that are covered by this Part do not apply to dwellings, the provisions may still be required in the situations described above in order to satisfy the Workplace Regulations.

MIXED USE DEVELOPMENT

In mixed use developments part of a building may be used as a dwelling while another part has a non-domestic use. In such cases, if the requirements of this part of the Regulations for dwellings and non-domestic use differ, the requirements for non-domestic use should apply in any shared parts of the building.

The Requirement

This Approved Document, which takes effect on 6 April 2006, deals with the requirement of Part F of Schedule 1 to the Building Regulations 2000.

This guidance does not apply to building work in circumstances where the amendments to Part L made by the Building and Approved Inspectors (Amendment) Regulations 2006 do not apply to the work.

Requirement	Limits on application
Means of Ventilation **F1.** There shall be adequate means of ventilation provided for people in the building.	Requirement F1 does not apply to a building or space within a building: a. into which people do not normally go; or b. which is used solely for storage; or c. which is a garage used solely in connection with a single dwelling.

Section 0: General guidance

Performance

0.1   In the Secretary of State's view the Requirement of Part F will be met where a ventilation system is provided that, under normal conditions, is capable of limiting the accumulation of moisture, which could lead to mould growth, and pollutants originating within a building which would otherwise become a hazard to the health of the people in the building.

0.2   In general terms, the requirement may be achieved by providing a ventilation system which:

a.   extracts, before it is generally widespread, water vapour from areas where it is produced in significant quantities (e.g. kitchens, utility rooms and bathrooms);

b.   extracts, before they are generally widespread, pollutants which are a hazard to health from areas where they are produced in significant quantities (e.g. rooms containing processes or activities which generate harmful contaminants);

c.   rapidly dilutes, when necessary, pollutants and water vapour produced in habitable rooms, occupiable rooms and sanitary accommodation;

d.   makes available over long periods a minimum supply of outdoor air for occupants and to disperse, where necessary, residual pollutants and water vapour. Such ventilation should minimise draughts and, where necessary, should be reasonably secure and provide protection against rain penetration;

e.   is designed, installed and commissioned to perform in a way which is not detrimental to the health of the people in the building; and

f.   is installed to facilitate maintenance where necessary.

0.3   The guidance in this Approved Document has not been formulated to deal with the products of tobacco smoking.

0.4   Ventilation systems in buildings result in energy being used to heat fresh air taken in from outside and, in mechanical ventilation systems, to move air into, out of and/or around the building. Energy efficiency is dealt with under Part L of the Building Regulations but consideration should be given to mitigation of ventilation energy use, where applicable, by employing heat recovery devices, efficient types of fan motor and/or energy-saving control devices in the ventilation system.

Introduction to the provisions

0.5   The purpose of this section is to outline briefly what ventilation in buildings is for and the philosophy behind the guidance for ventilation given in Approved Document F. More detail is given in some of the informative appendices at the end of this Approved Document.

The purpose of ventilation

0.6   Ventilation is simply the removal of 'stale' indoor air from a building and its replacement with 'fresh' outside air. It is assumed within the Approved Document that the outside air is of reasonable quality.

0.7   Ventilation is required for one or more of the following purposes:

a.   provision of outside air for breathing;

b.   dilution and removal of airborne pollutants, including odours;

c.   control of excess humidity (arising from water vapour in the indoor air);

d.   provision of air for fuel-burning appliances (which is covered under Part J of the Building Regulations).

Ventilation also provides a means to control thermal comfort and this, along with other methods, is considered in Part L of the Building Regulations and its supporting Approved Documents.

0.8   The airborne pollutants and water vapour mentioned in 0.7(b) and (c) above include those that are released from materials and products used in the construction, decoration and furnishing of a building, and as a result of the activities of the building's occupants.

0.9   The pollutant(s) of most importance will vary between building types (e.g. dwelling, office, factory), building uses (e.g. industrial process, shop, commercial kitchen), and even from room to room within a building (e.g. kitchen, shower room, conference room, photocopier room). Common pollutants in a dwelling are moisture and combustion products from unflued appliances (e.g. gas cookers) and chemical emissions from construction and consumer products. In an office building, body odour is often the key pollutant, but there are a number of other pollutant sources including the building itself, furnishings, printers and photocopiers.

Types of ventilation

0.10   Buildings are ventilated through a combination of infiltration and purpose-provided ventilation.

- Infiltration is the uncontrollable air exchange between the inside and outside of a building through a wide range of air leakage paths in the building structure.

- Purpose-provided ventilation is the controllable air exchange between the inside and outside of a building by means of a range of natural and/or mechanical devices.

0.11 It is important to minimise the uncontrollable infiltration and supply sufficient purpose-provided ventilation. Air tightness measures to limit infiltration are covered in Part L of the Building Regulations and its supporting Approved Documents. Approved Document F recommends methods of achieving sufficient purpose-provided ventilation, allowing for a reasonably high level of air tightness.

0.12 For the purposes of Part F, a reasonably high level of air tightness (air permeability) means a level higher than the target value recommended under Part L because all new buildings are expected to better the target value to some degree. Research suggests that the most airtight domestic and non-domestic buildings, using normal (but carefully executed) construction methods, can have an air permeability down to around 3–4m³/h per square metre of envelope area at 50 Pascal pressure difference. Therefore, the ventilation provisions recommended in this Approved Document have been specified to cope with air permeability at these levels or worse in typical building types. Where special measures are to be taken to achieve greater air tightness, additional ventilation provisions may be required.

The ventilation strategy adopted in Approved Document F

0.13 Approved Document F adopts the following strategy (systems which comply with the strategy are described in Sections 1 and 2).

- **Extract ventilation** from rooms where most water vapour and/or pollutants are released, e.g. activities such as cooking, bathing or photocopying. This is to minimise their spread to the rest of the building. This extract may be either intermittent or continuous.

- **Whole building ventilation** to provide fresh air to the building and to dilute and disperse residual water vapour and pollutants not dealt with by extract ventilation as well as removing water vapour and other pollutants which are released throughout the building (e.g. by building materials, furnishings, activities and the presence of occupants). Whole building ventilation provides nominally continuous air exchange. The ventilation rate may be reduced or ceased when the building is not occupied. It may be necessary to purge the air when the building is re-occupied.

- **Purge ventilation** throughout the building to aid removal of high concentrations of pollutants and water vapour released from occasional activities such as painting and decorating or accidental releases such as smoke from burnt food or spillage of water. Purge ventilation is intermittent, i.e. only required when such occasional activities occur. Purge ventilation provisions may also be used to improve thermal comfort and/or overheating of buildings in summer: the latter is considered further in Approved Documents L1(a) (New dwellings) and L2(a) (New buildings other than dwellings). Note that purge ventilation was called 'rapid'

ventilation in the 1995 edition of Approved Document F.

0.14 This ventilation strategy can be delivered by a natural ventilation system or a mechanical ventilation system or a combination of both (i.e. 'mixed-mode' or 'hybrid' ventilation system). For mainly naturally ventilated buildings, it is common to use a combination of ventilators to achieve this strategy (e.g. for dwellings it is common to use intermittent extraction fans for extract ventilation, trickle ventilators for whole building ventilation and windows for purge ventilation). For mechanically ventilated or air-conditioned buildings, it is common for the same ventilators to provide both local extract and whole building ventilation and, for buildings other than dwellings, to provide purge ventilation as well.

0.15 The ventilation systems and devices mentioned in the preceding paragraph are examples of those commonly in use at the time of writing. Other ventilation systems and devices, perhaps following a different strategy (e.g. positive input ventilation), may provide acceptable solutions, provided it can be demonstrated to the building control body (e.g. by a BBA Certificate) that they meet Requirement F1.

Control of ventilation

0.16 It is important that ventilation is controllable so that it can maintain reasonable indoor air quality and avoid waste of energy. These controls can be either manual (i.e. operated by the occupant) or automatic.

0.17 Manually controlled trickle ventilators (the most common type of background ventilators) can be located over the window frames, in window frames, just above the glass or directly through the wall (see Diagram 5 in the Glossary). They are positioned typically 1.7m above floor level to avoid discomfort due to cold draughts. These ventilators often incorporate a simple flap that allows users to shut off the ventilation provided depending on external weather conditions. Trickle ventilators are normally left open in occupied rooms in dwellings. A window with a night latch position is not recommended because of the difficulty of measuring the equivalent area, the greater likelihood of draughts and the potential increased security risk in some locations.

0.18 In dwellings, humidity controlled devices are available to regulate the humidity of the indoor air and, hence, minimise the risk of condensation and mould growth. These are best installed as part of an extract ventilator in moisture-generating rooms (e.g. kitchen or bathroom). Humidity control is not appropriate for sanitary accommodation where the dominant pollutant is normally odour. Trickle ventilators are available which 'throttle down' the ventilation flow passage(s) according to the pressure difference across the ventilator to reduce draught risks during windy weather. Manufacturers should be consulted when selecting the correct type of pressure-controlled trickle ventilator.

0.19 Other types of automatic control may be suitable for regulating ventilation devices (e.g. trickle ventilators, ventilation fans, dampers and air terminal devices) in dwellings. In such cases, it is important that the device controls the ventilation air supply and/or extract according to the need for ventilation in the space to remove or dilute indoor pollutants and water vapour. Trickle ventilators with automatic control should also have manual over-ride, so that the occupant can close the ventilator to avoid draughts and fully open the ventilator to provide maximum airflow when required. For pressure-controlled trickle ventilators that are fully open at typical conditions (e.g. 1Pa pressure difference), only a manual close option is recommended.

0.20 In buildings other than dwellings, various more sophisticated automatic control systems are available. These may be based on sensors located within the building, e.g. occupancy sensors (using local passive infra-red detectors) or indoor carbon dioxide concentration sensors (using electronic carbon dioxide detectors) as an indicator of occupancy level and, therefore, body odour.

Performance-based guidance

0.21 This Approved Document focuses on performance-based guidance which suggests to the designer what level of ventilation should be sufficient, rather than how it should be achieved. Therefore, the designer has the freedom to use whatever ventilation provisions suit a particular building, including the use of innovative products and solutions, if it can be demonstrated that they meet the performance standard recommended in this Approved Document.

0.22 The actual performance criteria for acceptable levels of moisture and pollutants are given in Appendix A. The airflow rates necessary to meet the performance criteria are given in the main guidance.

0.23 Simple guidance in the form of ventilator sizes for the whole dwelling is also provided to make it easier for designers to meet Building Regulations requirements in common situations.

Equivalent area and free area of ventilators

0.24 **Equivalent area** has been introduced into the Approved Document instead of **free area** for the sizing of background ventilators (including trickle ventilators). Equivalent area is a better measure of the airflow performance of a ventilator. Free area is simply the physical size of the aperture of the ventilator but may not accurately reflect the airflow performance which the ventilator will achieve. The more complicated and/or contorted the air flow passages in a ventilator, the less air will flow through it. So, two different ventilators with the same free area will not necessarily have the same airflow performance. A new European Standard, BS EN 13141-1:2004 (Clause 4), includes a method of measuring the equivalent area of background ventilator openings. As an approximation, the free area of a trickle ventilator is typically 25% greater than its equivalent area.

0.25 As equivalent area cannot be verified with a ruler, it will be difficult to demonstrate to building control bodies that trickle ventilators and similar products have the correct equivalent area unless it is clearly marked on the product. For this reason, it is preferable to use ventilators which have the equivalent area (in mm^2 at 1Pa pressure difference), or equivalent area per metre (where the equivalent area of the product varies according to length) marked on the product in an easily visible location. Where it is not practical for the manufacturer to mark the ventilator because it can be used in conjunction with a range of other components, some form of temporary marking for the installed system should be acceptable to the building control body.

0.26 Some manufacturers will not have developed marking, or equivalent, systems for their products by 6 April 2006. Therefore, until 1 October 2006 it would be reasonable for building control bodies to adopt a flexible approach to assessing equivalent area where unmarked products are used.

Ventilation effectiveness

0.27 Ventilation effectiveness is a measure of how well a ventilation system works in terms of delivering the supply air to the occupants of a building. If the supply air is mixed fully with the room air before it is breathed by the occupants, the ventilation effectiveness is 1. If the supply air is extracted from the room before it mixes with any room air, the ventilation effectiveness is 0. If the supply air reaches the occupant without mixing with any room air, the ventilation effectiveness tends towards infinity.

0.28 This is important as a system with a higher ventilation effectiveness achieves acceptable pollutant levels at the occupant's breathing zone for a lower air supply rate, and offers potentially significant energy savings. However, it has been decided not to make an allowance for any reduction of fresh air supply rates based on ventilation effectiveness in Approved Document F at this time. This is because ventilation effectiveness is dependent on the ventilation system design, its installation and the way in which occupants use the space. Whilst it is possible to predict what the ventilation effectiveness of a system should be, there is currently insufficient knowledge of the actual ventilation effectiveness achieved in buildings to allow designers to guarantee performance and so avoid significant under-ventilation by reducing air supply rates. This is because ventilation effectiveness may be influenced by factors beyond the designer's control such as occupant usage (e.g. seating plan and use of computers within a space and whether the space is being heated or cooled by the ventilation air). In the designs shown in this Approved Document, it has been assumed that the ventilation effectiveness is 1.0. See CIBSE Guide A for further information on ventilation effectiveness.

Source control

0.29 A complementary strategy for achieving good indoor air quality is to reduce the release of water vapour and/or air pollutants into the indoor air, i.e. source control. Source control is not considered within the main guidance of the Approved Document owing to limited knowledge about the emission of pollutants from construction and consumer products used in buildings and the lack of suitable labelling schemes for England and Wales. Some construction products such as glass, stone and ceramics are by their nature low emitters of air pollutants. Currently, some paints are labelled for their volatile organic compound (VOC) content, and some wood-based boards (class E1, BS EN 13986:2002) are available with low formaldehyde emission. This allows suitable products to be chosen when good indoor air quality is a priority, but at the present time it is not practical to make an allowance for use of these products in the ventilation requirements. Further information about control of emissions from construction products is available in BRE Digest 464.

0.30 House dust mite allergens can trigger allergic reactions in susceptible individuals. Measures for source control are provided in BRE Report BR 417: *Building regulation health and safety*.

Noisy locations

0.31 In noisy areas it may be appropriate to use either sound-attenuating background ventilators or mechanical ventilation solutions, depending on the noise level and any planning conditions.

Noise from ventilation systems

0.32 Noise generated by ventilation fans (which may propagate through ducts and ductwork) can disturb the occupants of the building and so discourage their use. Therefore, the designer should consider minimising noise by careful design and the specification of quieter products. Noise from the ventilation system may also disturb people outside the building, so externally emitted noise levels should also be considered.

Historic buildings

0.33 The inclusion of any particular ventilation measure in existing buildings should not introduce new or increased technical risk, or otherwise prejudice the use or character of the building. In particular, consideration should be given to the special needs of historic buildings. Such buildings include:

a. listed buildings;

b. buildings situated in a conservation area;

c. buildings of local architectural and historical interest and which are referred to as a material consideration in a local authority's development plan;

d. buildings within national parks, areas of outstanding natural beauty and world heritage sites.

0.34 Advice on the factors determining the character of historic buildings is set out in PPG15: *Planning and the historic environment*. Specific guidance on meeting the requirements of Part F when undertaking work in historic buildings is given in Section 3 of this Approved Document.

Modular and portable buildings

0.35 Buildings constructed from sub-assemblies that are delivered newly made or selected from stock are no different from any other new building and must comply with all requirements in Schedule 1 of the Building Regulations 2000. In some applications, such as buildings that are constructed to be temporary (in the normal sense of the word), the provision of adequate ventilation may vary depending upon the circumstances in the particular case. For example, (a) a building created by dismantling, transporting and re-erecting the sub-assemblies on the same premises would normally be considered to meet the requirements and (b) a building constructed from sub-assemblies obtained from other premises or from stock manufactured before this Approved Document came into force would normally be considered to meet the requirement if it satisfies the relevant requirements of Part F that were applicable in 1995.

Section 1: Dwellings

Introduction to provisions

1.1 This Approved Document shows three main ways of complying with the Requirement by:

a. providing the ventilation rates set out in paragraphs 1.4 to 1.7; or

b. following the system guidance set out:

- for dwellings without basements (paragraph 1.8); or

- for dwellings with basements (paragraphs 1.9 to 1.11); or

c. using other ventilation systems provided it can be demonstrated to the building control body that they satisfy the Requirement, e.g. by showing that they meet the moisture and air quality criteria set out in Appendix A.

1.2 There should be reasonable access for maintenance. This should include access for the purpose of changing filters, replacing defective components and cleaning duct work.

1.3 Note that extract fans lower the pressure in a building, which can cause the spillage of combustion products from open-flued appliances. This can occur even if the appliance and the fan are in different rooms. Ceiling sweep fans produce air currents and hence local depressurisation which can also cause the spillage of flue gases from open-flued gas appliances or from solid fuel open fires. In buildings where it is intended to install open-flued combustion appliances and extract fans, the combustion appliance should be able to operate safely whether or not the fans are running. A way of showing compliance in these circumstances would be to follow the guidance given in Approved Document J on both the installation of the appliances and tests to show that combustion appliances operate safely whether or not fans are running.

Ventilation rates

1.4 The performance will be achieved by providing the airflow rates set out in paragraphs 1.5 to 1.7. The airflow rates specified are for the performance of the complete installation. It is not intended that this should be measured on-site but the performance of the ventilation device (and associated components such as ducting for fans) should be tested according to the Standards listed under 'Performance requirements' in Table 1.6.

1.5 Extract ventilation to outside is required in each kitchen, utility room and bathroom and for sanitary accommodation. The extract can be either intermittent or continuously operating. The minimum extract airflow rates at the highest and lowest settings should be no less than specified in Table 1.1a.

1.6 Whole building ventilation rate for the supply of air to the habitable rooms in a dwelling should be no less than specified in Table 1.1b.

1.7 Purge ventilation provision is required in each habitable room (extract provisions are sufficient in other rooms, e.g. kitchens, bathrooms). It should be capable of extracting a minimum of four air changes per hour (ach) per room directly to outside.

Table 1.1a **Extract ventilation rates**

Room	Minimum intermittent extract rate	Continuous extract	
		Minimum high rate	**Minimum low rate**
Kitchen	30l/s (adjacent to hob); or 60l/s (elsewhere)	13l/s	Total extract rate must be at least the whole building ventilation rate in Table 1.1b
Utility room	30l/s	8l/s	
Bathroom	15l/s	8l/s	
Sanitary accommodation	6l/s		

Table 1.1b **Whole building ventilation rates**

	Number of bedrooms in dwelling				
	1	**2**	**3**	**4**	**5**
Whole building ventilation rate [a,b] (l/s)	13	17	21	25	29

Notes:

a. In addition, the minimum ventilation rate should be not less than 0.3l/s per m^2 internal floor area (this includes each floor, e.g. for a two-storey building, add the ground and first floor areas).

b. This is based on two occupants in the main bedroom and a single occupant in all other bedrooms. This should be used as the default value. If a greater level of occupancy is expected, then add 4l/s per occupant.

Ventilation systems for dwellings without basements

1.8   The performance required for dwellings without basements could be achieved by following steps 1 to 5. Worked examples for each system are given in Appendix C.

Step 1: Select **one** of the following four ventilation systems (illustrated in Diagram 1).

> **System 1: Background ventilators and intermittent extract fans**. Guidance on minimum provisions for extract and whole building ventilation is set out in Table 1.2a. Note that it includes separate guidance for dwellings with only a single exposed façade. See Appendix E for installation guidance for intermittent extract fans.

> **System 2: Passive stack ventilation**. Guidance on minimum provisions for extract and whole building ventilation is set out in Table 1.2b. See Appendix D for design and installation guidance for PSV.

> **System 3: Continuous mechanical extract**. Guidance on minimum provisions for extract and whole building ventilation is set out in Table 1.2c.

> **System 4: Continuous mechanical supply and extract with heat recovery**. Guidance on minimum provisions for extract and whole building ventilation is set out in Table 1.2d.

Step 2: See Table 1.3 for guidance on minimum provision for purge ventilation.

Step 3: See Table 1.4 for guidance on suitable ventilator locations (and minimum background ventilator areas for each room).

Step 4: See Table 1.5 for guidance on appropriate ventilation controls.

Step 5: See Table 1.6 for guidance on performance test methods.

Diagram 1 **Ventilation systems**

Background ventilators and intermittent extract fans

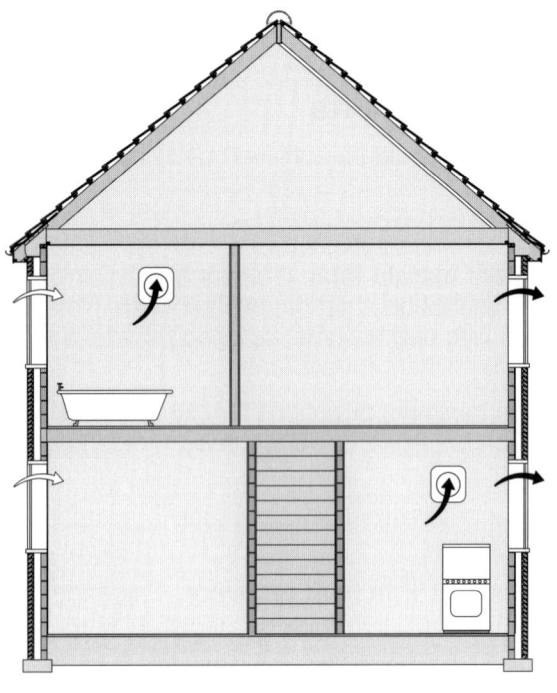

Passive stack ventilation

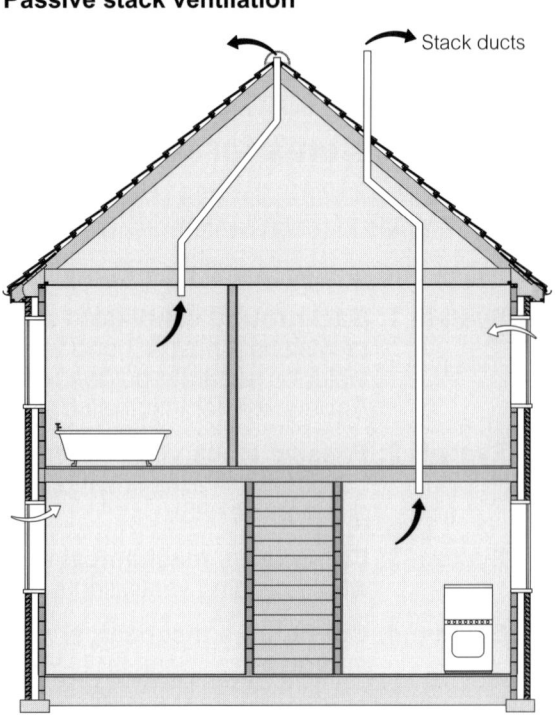

Stack ducts

Continuous mechanical extract

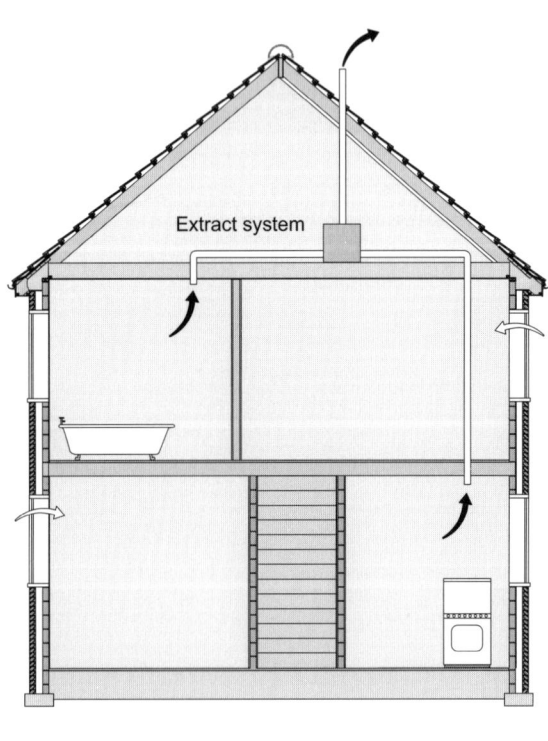

Extract system

Continuous mechanical supply and extract with heat recovery

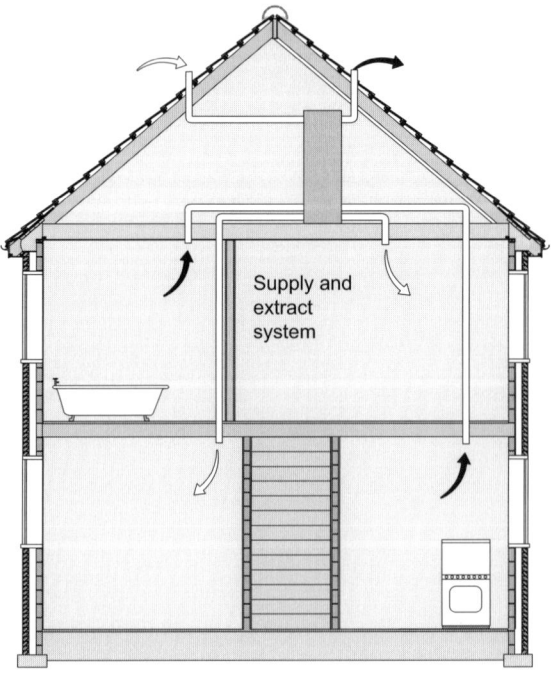

Supply and extract system

Table 1.2a System 1 – Background ventilators and intermittent extract fans (for additional information see Tables 1.3 to 1.6 and worked examples C1 and C5 in Appendix C)

Intermittent extract

- Intermittent extract rates are given in Table 1.1a. For sanitary accommodation only, as an alternative, the purge ventilation provisions (windows) given in Appendix B can be used where security is not an issue.

- Instead of a conventional intermittent fan, a continuously running single room heat recovery ventilator could be used in a wet room. It should use the minimum high rate in Table 1.1a and 50% of this value as the minimum low rate. No background ventilator is required in the same room as a single room heat recovery ventilator. Furthermore, the total equivalent background ventilator area described below can be reduced by 2500mm² for each room containing a single room heat recovery ventilator. Continuously running fans should be quiet so as not to discourage their use by the occupants.

Background ventilators

- For dwellings with more than one exposed façade:

    a. for multi-storey dwellings, and single-storey dwellings more than four storeys above ground level, the total equivalent area for the dwelling is given in the table below; or

    b. for single-storey dwellings, up to four storeys above ground level, take the total equivalent area for the dwelling from the table below and add 5000mm².

- For a dwelling with only a single exposed façade, cross ventilation is not possible using this type of ventilation system and an alternative is required. In this case, background ventilators should be located at both high and low positions in the façade to provide single-sided ventilation. The total equivalent area at a high position (typically 1.7m above floor level) for all dwelling types (i.e. all storey heights) is given in the main table. In addition, the same total equivalent ventilator area should be repeated and located at least 1.0m below the high ventilators. See Diagram 1b. Single-sided ventilation is most effective if the dwelling is designed so that the habitable rooms are on the exposed façade, and these rooms are no greater than 6m in depth.

Equivalent ventilator area[a] for dwellings (mm²)

Total floor area (m²)	Number of bedrooms[b]				
	1	**2**	**3**	**4**	**5**
≤ 50	25,000	35,000	45,000	45,000	55,000
51–60	25,000	30,000	40,000		
61–70	30,000	30,000	30,000		
71–80	35,000	35,000	35,000		
81–90	40,000	40,000	40,000		
91–100	45,000	45,000	45,000		
> 100	Add 5000mm² for every additional 10m² floor area				

Notes:

a. The equivalent area of a background ventilator should be determined at a 1Pa pressure difference, using the appropriate test method given in Table 1.6.

b. This is based on two occupants in the main bedroom and a single occupant in all other bedrooms. For a greater level of occupancy, assume greater number of bedrooms (i.e. assume an extra bedroom per additional person). For more than five bedrooms, add an additional 10,000mm² per bedroom.

Diagram 1b **Single-sided ventilation**

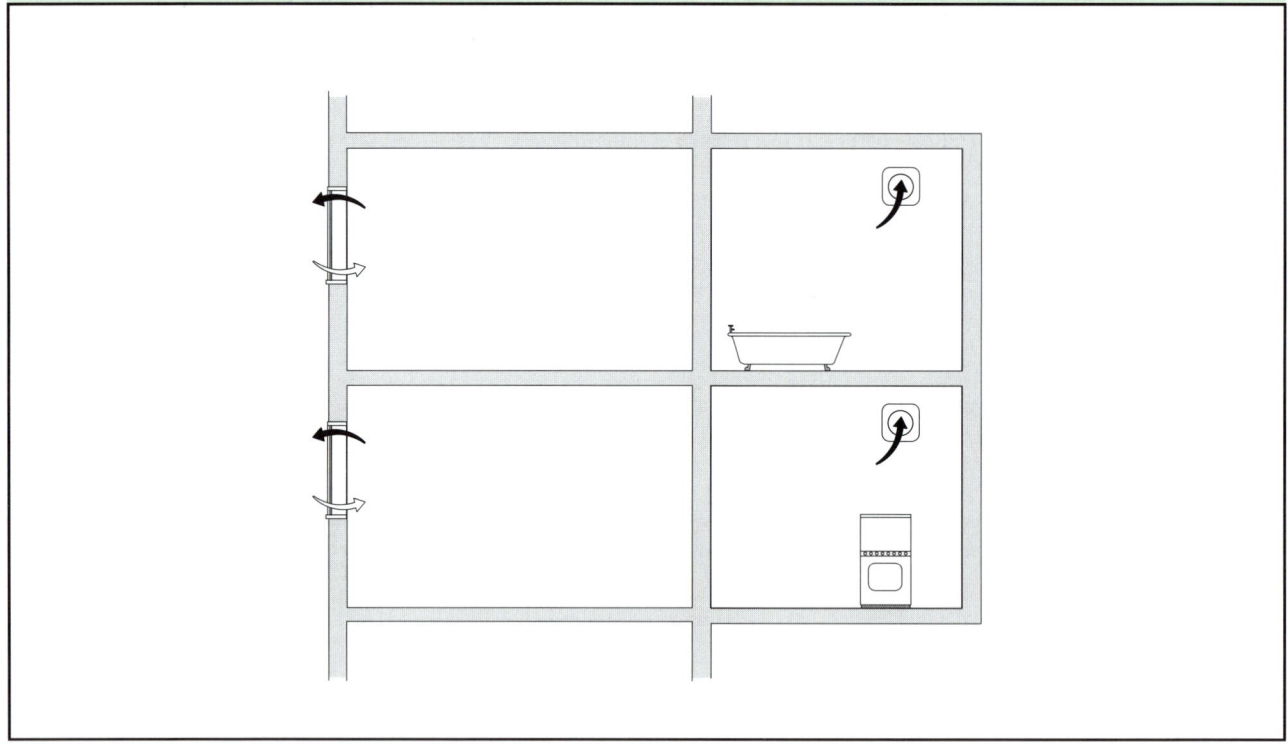

Table 1.2b **System 2 – Passive stack ventilation (for additional information see Tables 1.3 to 1.6 and worked examples C2 and C6 in Appendix C)**

Passive stack ventilators[a]

Room	Internal duct diameter (mm)	Internal cross sectional area (mm²)
Kitchen	125	12,000
Utility room	100	8000
Bathroom	100	8000
Sanitary accommodation[b]	80	5000

Background ventilators[c]

Calculate the total equivalent area of ventilators (mm²) required in the dwelling as follows:

Step 1: determine the equivalent ventilator area for the dwelling from Table 1.2a;

Step 2: make an allowance for the total airflow through all PSV units. As an approximation, assume that, under normal conditions, each PSV unit provides an equivalent ventilator area of 2500mm²;

Step 3: equivalent area required = step 1 – step 2.

Note that the minimum equivalent area (step 3) must always be at least equal to the total maximum cross-sectional area of all the PSV ducts to ensure sufficient make-up air for the PSV to operate fully. For a dwelling with only a single exposed façade, the dwelling should be designed such that the habitable rooms are on the exposed façade so as to achieve cross ventilation.

Notes:

a. An open-flued appliance may provide sufficient extract ventilation for the room in which it is located when in operation, and can be arranged to provide sufficient ventilation when not firing. For instance, the provisions would be adequate if: (a) the solid fuel open-flued appliance is a primary source of heating, cooking or hot water production; or (b) the open-flued appliance has a flue of free area at least equivalent to a 125mm diameter duct and the appliance's combustion air inlet and dilution inlet are permanently open, i.e. there is a path with no control dampers which could block the flow or the ventilation path can be left open when the appliance is not in use (see also paragraph 1.3).

b. For sanitary accommodation only, as an alternative, the purge ventilation provisions given in Appendix B can be used where security is not an issue.

c. In addition, use this procedure to calculate sizes of background ventilators if both PSV (or open-flued appliance as described in note a above) and intermittent extract fans are used in different rooms in the same dwelling. See also paragraph 1.3 if open-flued appliances are installed in the building.

Table 1.2c **System 3 – Continuous mechanical extract (for additional information see Tables 1.3 to 1.6 and worked examples C3 and C7 in Appendix C)**

Continuous extract

Step 1:   Determine the whole building ventilation rate from Table 1.1b.

(Note: no allowance is made for infiltration as the extract system lowers the pressure in the dwelling and limits the exit of air through the building fabric.)

Step 2:   Calculate the whole dwelling air extract rate at maximum operation by summing the individual room rates for 'minimum high rate' from Table 1.1a.

(For sanitary accommodation only, as an alternative, the purge ventilation provisions given in Appendix B can be used where security is not an issue. In this case the 'minimum high extract rate' for the sanitary accommodation should be omitted from the step 2 calculation.)

Step 3:   The required extract rates are as follows:

- the maximum rate (e.g. '**boost**') should be at least the greater of step 1 and step 2. Note that the maximum individual room extract rates should be at least those given in Table 1.1a for minimum high rate;

- the **minimum rate** should be at least the whole building ventilation rate in step 1.

Note 1: this system could comprise either a central extract system or individual room fans (or a combination of both). In all cases, the fans should operate quietly at their minimum (i.e. normal) rate so as not to discourage their use (see paragraph 0.31). To ensure that the system provides the intended ventilation rate, measures should be taken to minimise likely wind effects when any extract terminal is located on the prevailing windward façade. Possible solutions include ducting to another façade, use of constant volume flow rate units or, for central extract systems, follow more detailed guidance which is being prepared by the Energy Saving Trust (EST) and the Building Research Establishment (BRE) in conjunction with The Electric Heating and Ventilation Association (TEHVA) and the Residential Ventilation Association (RVA) entitled 'Performance testing of products for residential ventilation' (to be published in February/March 2006 and will be made available on their websites).

Note 2: if a single room heat recovery ventilator (SRHRV) is used to ventilate a habitable room, with the rest of the dwelling provided with continuous mechanical extract, the airflow rates are determined as follows:

- determine the whole building ventilation rate from Table 1.1b;

- calculate the room supply rate required for the SRHRV from: (whole building ventilation rate x room volume) / (total volume of all habitable rooms).

Undertake steps 1 to 3 for sizing the continuous mechanical extract for the rest of the dwelling. However, when performing step 1, the supply rate specified for the SRHRV should be subtracted from the value given in Table 1.1b.

Background ventilators

The need for background ventilators will depend on the air permeability of the dwelling, and this is not normally known at the design stage. Therefore, as a precaution, it is recommended that controllable background ventilators having a minimum equivalent area of 2500mm² are fitted in each room, except wet rooms from which air is extracted. Where this approach causes difficulties (e.g. on a noisy site) seek expert advice.

Table 1.2d System 4 – Continuous mechanical supply and extract with heat recovery (MVHR) (for additional information see Tables 1.3 to 1.6 and worked examples C4 and C8 in Appendix C)

Continuous supply and extract

Step 1: Determine the whole building ventilation rate from Table 1.1b. Allow for infiltration by subtracting from this value:

- for multi-storey dwellings: 0.04 x gross internal volume of the dwelling heated space (m^3);
- for single-storey dwellings: 0.06 x gross internal volume of the dwelling heated space (m^3).

Step 2: Calculate the whole dwelling air extract rate at maximum operation by summing the individual room rates for 'minimum high rate' from Table 1.1a.

(For sanitary accommodation only, as an alternative, the purge ventilation provisions given in Appendix B can be used where security is not an issue. In this case the 'minimum high extract rate' for the sanitary accommodation should be omitted from the step 2 calculation.)

Step 3: The required airflow rates are as follows:

- the maximum extract rate (e.g. 'boost') should be at least the greater of step 1 and step 2. Note that the maximum individual room extract rates should be at least those given in Table 1.1a for minimum high rate;
- the minimum air supply rate should be at least the whole building ventilation rate in step 1.

Table 1.3 Purge ventilation provisions for all four ventilation systems

Purge ventilation

For each habitable room with:

- external walls, see Appendix B for window or external door (including patio door) sizing;
- no external walls, see paragraphs 1.12 to 1.14.

There may be practical difficulties in achieving this (e.g. owing to excessive noise from outside). In such situations, seek expert advice.

For each wet room with:

- external walls, install an openable window (no minimum size);
- no external walls, the normal extract provisions will suffice, although it will take longer to purge the room (see Table 1.5 for intermittent extract use in System 1).

Table 1.4 **Location of ventilation devices in rooms**

Mechanical (intermittent and continuous) extract or supply

- Cooker hoods should be 650 to 750mm above the hob surface (or follow manufacturer's instructions).

- Mechanical extract terminals and extract fans should be placed as high as practicable and preferably less than 400mm below the ceiling.

- Mechanical supply terminals should be located and directed to avoid draughts.

- Where ducts etc. are provided in a dwelling with a protected stairway, precautions may be necessary to avoid the possibility of the system allowing smoke or fire to spread into the stairway. See Approved Document B.

- The fans or terminals should be located in the following rooms:

  - **System 1:** extract should be from each wet room.

  - **System 3:** extract should be from each wet room.

  - **System 4:** extract should be from each wet room. Air should normally be supplied to each habitable room. The total supply airflow should usually be distributed in proportion to the habitable room volumes. Recirculation by the system of moist air from the wet rooms to the habitable rooms should be avoided.

Passive stack ventilation

- PSV extract terminals should be located in the ceiling or on a wall less than 400mm below the ceiling. There should be no background ventilators within the same room as a PSV terminal. (For open-flued appliances, room air supply is necessary as given in Approved Document J.)

- Where PSV is provided in a dwelling with a protected stairway, precautions may be necessary to avoid the possibility of the system allowing smoke or fire to spread into the stairway. See Approved Document B.

Background ventilators

- They should be located in the following rooms:

  - **System 1:** located in all rooms. Minimum of 5000mm^2 equivalent area in all habitable rooms with an external wall. If a habitable room has no external walls, follow guidance in paragraphs 1.12 to 1.14. Minimum of 2500mm^2 equivalent area in all wet rooms with an external wall. If a wet room has no external walls, follow the guidance for mechanical intermittent extract in Table 1.5. The total equivalent area should be at least that given in Table 1.2a. Where background ventilators and individual fans are fitted in the same room, they should be a minimum of 0.5m apart.

  - **System 2:** located in all rooms except within the same room as a passive stack ventilator. Minimum of 5000mm^2 in all habitable rooms with an external wall (with total at least that given in Table 1.2b). If a habitable room has no external walls, follow guidance in paragraphs 1.12 to 1.14.

  - **System 3:** located in each habitable room (see Table 1.2c).

  - **System 4:** no background ventilators required.

- In addition, background ventilators should be:

  - **All systems:** located so as to avoid draughts, e.g. typically 1.7m above floor level. For System 1, if dwelling has a single exposed façade, the low ventilators should be below this level (see Table 1.2a).

  - **Systems 1 and 2:** if the dwelling has more than one exposed façade, to maximise the airflow through the dwelling by encouraging cross ventilation, it is best to locate similar equivalent areas of background ventilators on opposite (or adjacent) sides of the dwelling.

Note that, for Systems 1 and 2, the background ventilators have been sized for the winter period. Additional ventilation may be required during warmer months as stack driving pressures are reduced. The provisions for purge ventilation (e.g. windows) could be used. Additional background ventilation provision or the use of Systems 3 or 4 may be more appropriate for dwellings designed to high air tightness standards. If uncertain, seek expert advice.

Purge ventilation

- Location not critical.

Air transfer between rooms

- To ensure good transfer of air throughout the dwelling, there should be an undercut of minimum area 7600mm^2 in all internal doors above the floor finish (equivalent to an undercut of 10mm for a standard 760mm width door).

Table 1.5 **Controls for ventilation devices**

Mechanical intermittent extract

Intermittent extract can be operated manually and/or automatically by a sensor (e.g. humidity sensor, occupancy/usage sensor, detection of moisture/pollutant release). Humidity controls should not be used for sanitary accommodation as odour is the main pollutant.

In kitchens, any automatic control must provide sufficient flow during cooking with fossil fuels (e.g. gas) to avoid the build-up of combustion products.

Any automatic control must provide manual over-ride to allow the occupant to turn the extract on.

For a room with no openable window (i.e. an internal room), the fan should have a 15 minute over-run. In rooms with no natural light, the fans could be controlled by the operation of the main room light switch.

Mechanical continuous supply or extract/passive stack ventilation

Set up to operate without occupant intervention (may have manual control to select maximum 'boost' rate). May have automatic controls. (e.g. humidity sensor, occupancy/usage sensor, detection of moisture/pollutant release). Humidity controls should not be used for sanitary accommodation as odour is the main pollutant.

In kitchens, any automatic control must provide sufficient flow during cooking with fossil fuels (e.g. gas) to avoid the build-up of combustion products.

Ensure the system always provides the minimum whole building ventilation provision as specified in Table 1.1b.

Background ventilators

They can be either manually adjustable or automatically controlled (see paragraphs 0.17 to 0.19).

Purge ventilation

Manually operated.

Accessible controls

Where manual controls are provided, they should be within reasonable reach of occupants. It is recommended that they are located in accordance with the guidance for Requirement N3 *Safe opening and closing of windows etc.*, which is given in Approved Document N. Where reasonable, the use of pull cords, operating rods or similar devices may help to achieve this. Although Requirement N3 only applies to work places, for the purposes of this Approved Document it should also apply to dwellings.

Table 1.6 **Performance test methods**

The minimum performance requirements specified within Table 1.2 (a-d) for each ventilator, should be assessed using the test methods contained in relevant clauses of the following documents:

i. Intermittent extract fan

- BS EN 13141-4 Clause 4 'Performance testing of aerodynamic characteristics'. All sub-clauses are relevant.

ii. Range hood

- BS EN 13141-3 Clause 4 'Performance testing of aerodynamic characteristics'. All sub-clauses are relevant.

iii. Background ventilator (non-RH controlled)

- BS EN 13141-1 Clause 4 'Performance testing of aerodynamic characteristics'. Only the following sub-clauses are relevant:

  a. 4.1 'Flow rate/pressure'; and

  b. 4.2 'Non-reverse flow ability'.

  The performance requirement should normally be met for both airflow from outside to inside the dwelling and for inside to outside. To ensure the installed performance of background ventilators is similar to the results achieved when they are tested to this Standard, background ventilators and associated components should be installed according to manufacturers' instructions. This also applies to non-RH-controlled sound-attenuating background ventilators.

iv. Passive stack ventilator

- Follow Appendix D.

v. Continuous mechanical extract ventilation (MEV) system

- BS EN 13141-6 Clause 4 'Performance testing of aerodynamic characteristics'. Also see Note 2 below.

vi. Continuous supply and the extract ventilation MVHR unit

- BS EN 13141-7 Clause 6 'Test methods'. Also see Note 2 below.

vii. Single room heat recovery ventilator

- prEN 13141-8 Clause 6 ' Test methods'. Only the following sub-clauses are relevant:

  a. 6.1 'General'; and

  b. 6.2 'Performance testing of aerodynamic characteristics' sub-sub-clauses 6.2.1 'Leakages and mixing' and 6.2.2 'Airflow' only.

  Note: for internal and external leakage and for mixing, the until should meet at least Class U4 given in Clause 3.2 'Classification'.

Note 1: for all ventilators discussed in this Table, the fitting of ducting, intake/exhaust terminals, filters, etc. will impose an additional resistance to the airflow through a ventilation device such as a fan, cooker hood or supply and extract ventilation unit. Where appropriate this should be allowed for when specifying ventilation system components because, for example a fan that meets the requirement in Table 1.2 when tested on its own many fail to meet the requirement when it is installed and fitted with ducting and intake/exhaust grilles. In such cases, the performance of the separate components should be assessed according to the relevant parts of BS EN 13141 and other relevant Standards, and the complete assembly, as installed, designed to meet the performance requirement by following good practice such as is given in the CIBSE Guides. Also see Appendix E for installation guidance for intermittent fans.

Note 2: Detailed guidance on the tests to be undertaken is being prepared by the Energy Saving Trust (EST) and the Building Research Establishment (BRE) in conjunction with The Electric Heating and Ventilation Association (TEHVA) and the Residential Ventilation Association (RVA) entitled 'Performance testing of products for residential ventilation' (to be published in February/March 2006 and will be made available on their websites).

Ventilation systems for basements

1.9 For a dwelling which includes a basement that is connected to the rest of the dwelling above ground by a large permanent opening (e.g. an open stairway), the whole dwelling including the basement should be ventilated in accordance with paragraph 1.8 (for dwellings without basements) and treated as a multi-storey dwelling. If the basement has only a single exposed façade, while the rest of the dwelling above ground has more than one exposed façade, ventilation systems 3 and 4 are preferred, following the guidance in paragraph 1.8. If systems 1 or 2 are to be used, seek expert advice.

1.10 For a dwelling which includes a basement that is not connected to the rest of the dwelling above ground by a large permanent opening:

a. the part of the dwelling above ground should be considered separately and ventilated in accordance with paragraph 1.8. If the part of the dwelling above ground has no bedrooms, assume it has one bedroom for the purpose of determining ventilation provisions; and

b. the basement should be treated separately as a single-storey dwelling above ground in accordance with paragraph 1.8. If the basement has no bedrooms, assume it has one bedroom for the purpose of determining ventilation provisions.

1.11 For a dwelling which comprises only a basement it should be treated as a single-storey dwelling above ground in accordance with paragraph 1.8.

Ventilation of habitable rooms through another room or a conservatory

1.12 In a habitable room not containing openable windows (i.e. an internal room) the requirement will be met if the room is either ventilated through another habitable room (see paragraph 1.13) or through a conservatory (see paragraph 1.14).

1.13 A habitable room not containing openable windows may be ventilated through another habitable room (see Diagram 2) if:

a. there is, from the habitable rooms to outside, provision for both:

   i. **purge ventilation**, one or more ventilation openings, with a total area given in Diagram 2 based on at least the combined floor area of the habitable rooms; and

   ii. **background ventilation** of at least 8000mm^2 equivalent area; and

b. there is an area of permanent opening between the two rooms given in Diagram 2 based on at least the combined floor area of the habitable rooms.

1.14 A habitable room not containing openable windows may be ventilated through a conservatory (see Diagram 3) if:

a. there is, from the conservatory to outside, provisions for both:

   i. **purge ventilation**, one or more ventilation openings, with a total area given in Diagram 3 based on at least the combined floor area of the habitable room and conservatory; and

   ii. **background ventilation**, a ventilation opening (or openings) of at least 8000mm^2 equivalent area; and

b. there are openings (which must be closable) between the habitable room and the conservatory for:

   i. **purge ventilation** equivalent to 1.14a(i) above; and

   ii. **background ventilation** equivalent to 1.14a(ii) above which should be located typically at least 1.7m above floor level and need not be within the door frame.

Diagram 2 **Two habitable rooms treated as a single room for ventilation purposes**

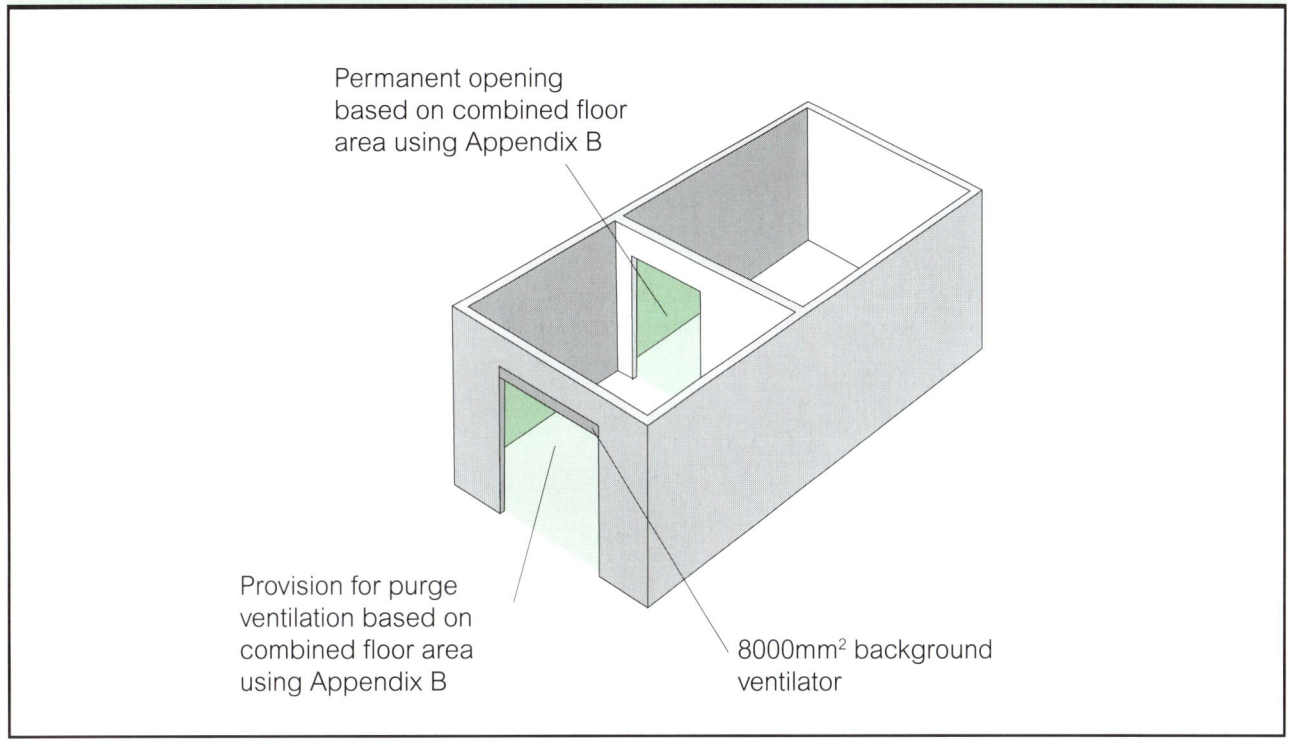

Permanent opening based on combined floor area using Appendix B

Provision for purge ventilation based on combined floor area using Appendix B

8000mm² background ventilator

Diagram 3 **A habitable room ventilated through a conservatory**

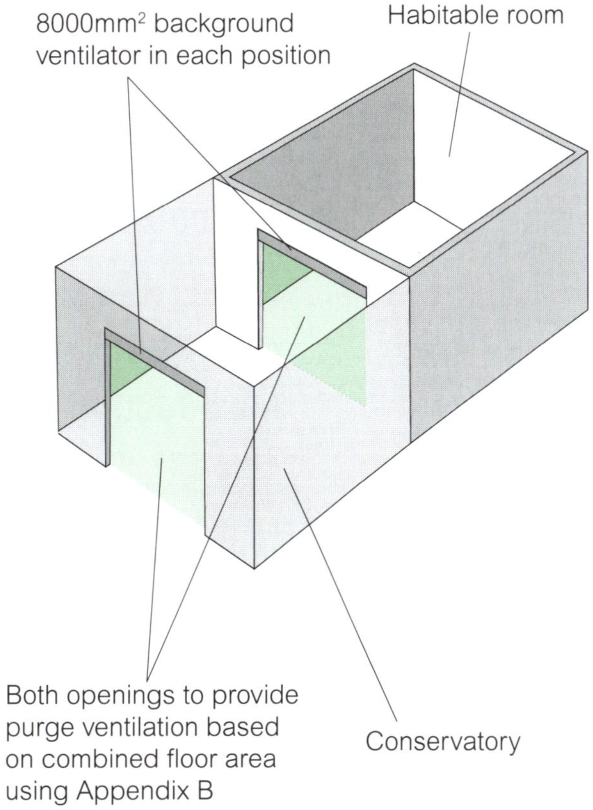

8000mm² background ventilator in each position

Habitable room

Both openings to provide purge ventilation based on combined floor area using Appendix B

Conservatory

Section 2: Buildings other than dwellings

General

2.1 This Approved Document sets out guidance for the following range of building types and uses:

a. offices – paragraphs 2.9 to 2.17;

b. car parks – paragraphs 2.19 to 2.22;

c. other building types – paragraph 2.18.

2.2 The ventilation provisions will not necessarily meet cooling needs. Guidance on the control of overheating is considered in Approved Document L2A *New buildings other than dwellings.*

2.3 Provision should be made to protect the fresh air supplies from contaminants injurious to health. Guidance on the siting of air inlets is provided in Appendix F.

2.4 Guidance on design measures to avoid *legionella* contamination, including design features not related to the ventilation of the building, is covered by HSE in *Legionnaires' disease: the control of legionella bacteria in water systems.* The relevant paragraphs are 79 to 144. Further guidance may be found in CIBSE TM13: *Minimising the risk of Legionnaires' disease.*

2.5 Guidance on recirculated air in air conditioning and mechanical ventilation systems is given by HSE in Workplace (Health, Safety and Welfare) Regulations 1992 *Approved Code of Practice and Guidance* L24, the relevant paragraph is 32.

Access for maintenance

2.6 Reasonable provision would be to include:

a. access for the purpose of replacing filters, fans and coils; and

b. provision of access points for cleaning duct work.

2.7 In a central plant room adequate space should be provided as necessary for the maintenance of the plant. Where no special provision is required, the requirement could be satisfied if 600mm space is provided where access is required between plant and 1100mm where space for routine cleaning is required (see Diagram 4). These figures are the minimum necessary and additional space may be needed for opening of access doors, withdrawal of filters, etc. Further guidance for more complex situations can be found in Defence Works Functional Standard, Design & Maintenance Guide 08: *Space requirements for plant access operation and maintenance.* Further guidance for the cleaning of ducts is provided by CIBSE *Ventilation hygiene toolkit.*

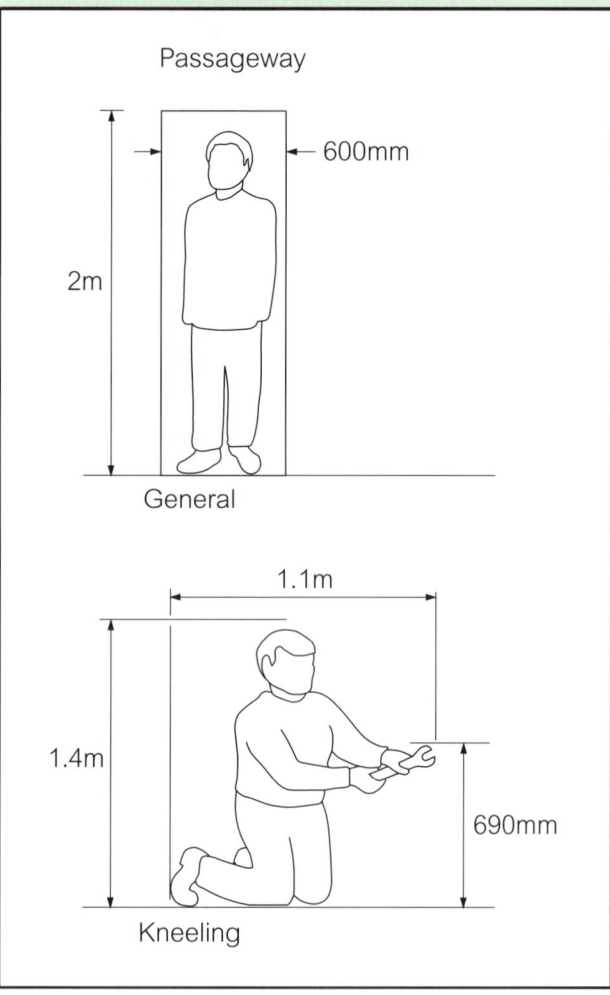

Diagram 4 **Spaces for access**

Passageway

600mm

2m

General

1.1m

1.4m

690mm

Kneeling

Commissioning

2.8 See Approved Document L2A *New buildings other than dwellings.*

OFFICES

Introduction to provisions

2.9 This Approved Document shows four main ways of complying with the requirement by:

a. providing ventilation which meets the airflow rates set out in paragraphs 2.10 to 2.14; or

b. following the system guidance set out in paragraphs 2.15 to 2.17; or

c. using the alternative approaches set out in paragraph 2.18;

d. using other ventilation systems provided it can be demonstrated to the building control body that they satisfy the Requirement, e.g. by showing that they meet the moisture and air quality criteria set out in Appendix A.

Ventilation rates

2.10 The performance will be achieved by ventilation which provides the airflow rates set out in paragraphs 2.11 to 2.14. The airflow rates specified are for the installed performance.

2.11 Extract to outside is required in all office sanitary accommodation, washrooms and in food and beverage preparation areas. In addition, printers and photocopiers in substantial use (greater than 30 minutes per hour) should be located in a separate room (to avoid any pollutants entering the occupied space) and extract provision installed. The extract flow rates should be no less than those specified in Table 2.1a.

2.12 The whole building ventilation rate for the supply of air to the offices should be no less than that specified in Table 2.1b.

2.13 Purge ventilation provision is required in each office. The total ventilation should be sufficient to reduce pollutants to an acceptable level before the space is occupied. The purged air should be taken directly to outside and should not be recirculated to any other part of the building.

2.14 The outdoor air supply rates in Table 2.1b for offices are based on controlling body odours with low levels of other pollutants. Where there are significant levels of other pollutants, adequate outdoor air supply can be achieved by following the calculation method provided in CIBSE Guide A.

Natural ventilation of rooms

2.15 The airflow rates specified in Tables 2.1a and 2.1b can be provided by a mainly natural ventilation system by following the guidance in Tables 2.2a, 2.2b and 2.2c. A wide range of natural ventilation systems for providing whole building ventilation is given in CIBSE Application Manual AM 10: *Natural ventilation in non-domestic buildings*.

Table 2.1a **Extract ventilation rates**

Room	Extract rate
Rooms containing printers and photocopiers in substantial use (greater than 30 minutes per hour)	Air extract rate of 20l/s per machine during use. Note that, if the operators are in the room continuously, use the greater of the extract and whole building ventilation rates
Office sanitary accommodation and washrooms	Intermittent air extract rate of: 15l/s per shower/bath 6l/s per WC/urinal
Food and beverage preparation areas (not commercial kitchens)	Intermittent air extract rate of: 15l/s with microwave and beverages only 30l/s adjacent to the hob with cooker(s) 60l/s elsewhere with cooker(s) All to operate while food and beverage preparation is in progress
Specialist buildings and spaces (e.g. commercial kitchens, sports centres)	See Table 2.3

Table 2.1b **Whole building ventilation rate for air supply to offices**

	Air supply rate
Total outdoor air supply rate for offices (no smoking and no significant pollutant sources)	10l/s per person

Mechanical ventilation of rooms

2.16   The requirement will be satisfied by following:

- the airflow rates set out in paragraphs 2.10 to 2.14; and

- the location guidance in Table 2.2b for extract ventilation; and

- the control guidance in Table 2.2c for extract ventilation.

Alternative approaches

2.17   As an alternative to paragraphs 2.10 to 2.14 the requirement will be satisfied by following the relevant recommendations of:

a.   CIBSE Application Manual AM 13: 2000: *Mixed mode ventilation*.

b.   CIBSE Guide A and CIBSE Guide B2.

Table 2.2 **Ventilation for offices with natural air supply**

a. Ventilation provisions

Extract

Extract rates as per paragraph 2.11[1, 2]

Whole building ventilation

See CIBSE Application Manual AM10:2005 *Natural ventilation in non-domestic buildings*.

Purge ventilation

See CIBSE Application Manual AM10:2005 *Natural ventilation in non-domestic buildings*.

Notes:

1. PSV can be used as an alternative to a mechanical extract fan for office sanitary and washrooms and food preparation areas.

2. When an open-flued appliance is provided in a building with mechanical extract, the spillage of flue gases could occur. The open-flued appliance needs to operate safely whether or not the fan is running, and further guidance is provided in Approved Document J.

---

b. Location of ventilators in rooms

Extract

- Extract ventilators should be located as high as practicable and preferably less than 400mm below the ceiling. This will tend to remove pollutants from the breathing zone of the occupants as well as increase the effectiveness of extracting buoyant pollutants and water vapour.

- For PSV, extract terminals should be located in the ceiling of the room.

Whole building ventilation

- See CIBSE Application Manual AM10:2005 *Natural ventilation in non-domestic buildings*.

Purge ventilation

- See CIBSE Application Manual AM10:2005 *Natural ventilation in non-domestic buildings*.

---

c. Controls for ventilators in rooms

Extract

- For extract fans, they can be controlled either manually or automatically. For a room with no openable window (i.e. an internal room), the extract should have a 15 minute over-run.

- For PSV, either operated manually and/or automatically by a sensor or controller.

Whole building ventilation

- See CIBSE Application Manual AM10:2005 *Natural ventilation in non-domestic buildings*.

Purge ventilation

- See CIBSE Application Manual AM10:2005 *Natural ventilation in non-domestic buildings*.

Accessible controls

- Readily accessible over-ride controls should be provided for the occupants.

VENTILATION OF OTHER TYPES OF BUILDINGS

2.18 The requirement will be satisfied by following the appropriate design guidance for the other buildings given in Table 2.3. In addition to the guidance documents listed below, it should be noted that the Workplace (Health, Safety, Welfare) Regulations 1992 apply to most places where people work.

Table 2.3 **Ventilation of other buildings and spaces**

Building/space/activity	Regulations and guidance
Animal husbandry	The Welfare of Farm Animals (England) Regulations SI 2000 No. 1870 London: The Stationery Office 2000.
	The Welfare of Farm Animals (England) (Amendment) Regulations SI 2002 No.1646
	The Welfare of Farm Animals (England) (Amendment) Regulations SI 2003 No. 299
	BS 5502 Buildings and Structures for Agriculture
	See also CIBSE Guide B2:2001, Section 3.24.1
Assembly halls	CIBSE Guide B2:2001, Section 3.3
Atria	CIBSE Guide B2:2001, Section 3.4
Broadcasting studios	CIBSE Guide B2:2001, Section 3.5
Building services plant rooms	Provision for emergency ventilation to control dispersal of contaminating gas releases (e.g. refrigerant leak) is given in paragraphs 23–25 of HSE Guidance Note HSG 202 *General Ventilation in the Workplace – Guidance for Employers*. Other guidance in BS 4434:1989 *Specification for safety aspects in the design, construction and installation of refrigeration appliances and systems*
Call centres	CIBSE Guide B2:2001, Section 3.24.2
Catering (inc. commercial kitchens)	HSE Catering Information Sheet No. 10, 2000: *Ventilation of kitchens in catering establishments*
	HSE Information Sheet No. 11, 2000: *The main health and safety law applicable to catering*
	See also CIBSE Guide B2:2001, Section 3.6
Cleanrooms	CIBSE Guide B2:2001, Section 3.7
Common spaces	These provisions apply to common spaces where large numbers of people are expected to gather, such as shopping malls and foyers. It does not apply to common spaces used solely or principally for circulation.
	The provision will be satisfied if there is provision to spaces where large numbers of people are expected to gather for either:
	a. natural ventilation by appropriately located ventilation opening(s) with a total opening area of at least 1/50th of the floor area of the common space; or
	b. mechanical ventilation installed to provide a supply of fresh air of 1l/s per m² of floor area
Communal residential buildings	Energy Efficiency Best Practice in Housing, Good Practice Guide GPG 192: *Designing energy efficient multi-residential buildings*
	See also CIBSE Guide B2:2001, Section 3.8
Computer rooms	CIBSE B2:2001, Section 3.9

Table 2.3 (continued) **Ventilation of other buildings and spaces**

Court rooms	Department for Constitutional Affairs *Court standards and Design Guide*, 2004
Darkrooms (photographic)	CIBSE Guide B2:2001, Section 3.24.4
Dealing rooms	CIBSE Guide B2:2001, Section 3.24.5
Factories and warehouses	Factories Act
	Health and Safety at Work etc. Act.
	See also CIBSE B2:2001, Section 3.11
	Requirements are often exceeded by other criteria such as the ventilation requirements of the particular manufacturing process
High-rise (non-domestic buildings)	CIBSE Guide B2:2001, Section 3.12
Horticulture	CIBSE Guide B2:2001, Section 2.42.6
Hospitals and healthcare buildings	NHS Activity database
	Health Technical Memorandum (HTM) 03
	Health Building Notes (HBN) – various
	CIBSE B2:2001, Section 3.13
Hotels	CIBSE Guide B2:2001, Section 3.14
Industrial ventilation	*Industrial Ventilation*, 24th Edition, *Manual of Recommended Practice*, American Conference of Government Industrial Hygienists
	HS(G) 37 An introduction to local exhaust ventilation
	HS(G) 54 Maintenance, Examination and Testing of Local Exhaust Ventilation
	HS(G) 193 COSHH Essentials
Laboratories	CIBSE Guide B2:2001, Section 3.16
Museums, libraries and art galleries	BS 5454:2000.
	CIBSE B2:2001, Section 3.17
Plant rooms	CIBSE Guide B2: Section 3.18
Prison cells	Refer to National Offender Management Service (NOMS). Home Office, NOMS Property, Technical Services, Room 401, Abell House, John Islip St., London SW1P 4LH
Schools and educational buildings	Ventilation provisions in schools can be made in accordance with the guidance in DfES Building Bulletin 101, *Ventilation of School Buildings* (see www.teachernet.gov.uk/iaq) and in the Education (School Premises) Regulations. Building Bulletin 101 can also be used as a guide to the ventilation required in other educational buildings such as further education establishments where the accommodation is similar to that found in schools, for e.g. sixth form accommodation. However, the standards may not be appropriate for particular areas where more hazardous activities take place than are normally found in schools, e.g. some practical and vocational activities requiring containment or fume extraction
	The Building Bulletin can also be used for children's centres and other early years settings, including day nurseries, playgroups, etc.
Shops and retail premises	CIBSE Guide B2:2001, Section 3.20
Sports centres (inc. swimming pools)	CIBSE Guide B2:2001, Section 3.21
Standards rooms	CIBSE Guide B2:2001, Section 3.24.7
Sanitary accommodation	Same as for offices in Table 2.1a
Transportation buildings and facilities	CIBSE Guide B2:2001, Section 3.23

VENTILATION OF CAR PARKS

2.19   The requirement will be satisfied for car parks below ground level, enclosed-type car parks and multi-storey car parks if the mean predicted pollutant levels are calculated and the ventilation rate designed and equipment installed to limit the concentration of carbon monoxide to not more than 30 parts per million averaged over an 8 hour period and peak concentrations, such as by ramps and exits, not more than 90 parts per million for periods not exceeding 15 minutes.

2.20   Note that Approved Document B also includes provision for the ventilation of car parks for the purpose of fire risk management.

Alternative approaches for ventilation of car parks

2.21   As an alternative to paragraph 2.20, the following guidance would satisfy the requirement:

a.   Naturally ventilated car parks. The provision of well-distributed permanent natural ventilation, e.g. openings at each car parking level with an aggregate equivalent area equal to at least 1/20th of the floor area at that level, of which at least 25% should be on each of two opposing walls.

b.   Mechanically ventilated car parks

Either:

   i.   the provision of both permanent natural ventilation openings of equivalent area not less than 1/40th of the floor area and a mechanical ventilation system capable of at least three air changes per hour (ach); or

   ii.   for basement car parks, the provision of a mechanical ventilation system capable of at least six air changes per hour (ach).

And:

For exits and ramps, where cars queue inside the building with engines running, provisions should be made to ensure a local ventilation rate of at least 10 air changes per hour (ach).

2.22   Further guidance can be found in *Code of practice for ground floor, multi-storey and underground car parks* published by the Association for Petroleum and Explosives Administration (www.apea.org.uk); CIBSE Guide B2, Section 3.23.3; and Health and Safety Publication EH40: *Occupational exposure limits for limiting concentration of exhaust pollutants*. Fire safety issues are considered in Approved Document B.

Section 3: Work on existing buildings

General

3.1 When building work is carried out on an existing building the work should comply with the applicable requirements of Schedule 1 of the Building Regulations 2000 (as amended) and the rest of the building should not be made less satisfactory in relation to the requirements than before the work was carried out (see Building Regulations 3 and 4). Further, when a building undergoes a Material Change of Use, as defined in Regulations 5 and 6 of the Building Regulations 2000 (as amended), Part F applies to the building, or that part of the building, which has been subject to the change of use. Therefore, the guidance in other sections of this Approved Document may be applicable.

3.2 Until 1 October 2006, to comply with requirement F1, it will be sufficient if replacement windows comply with the guidance in Table 1 or Table 2 of Approved Document F 1995. Also, until this date, replacement windows need only have trickle ventilators (or an equivalent form of ventilation) where the original windows had them.

3.3 Windows are a controlled fitting (see Regulation 3(1) and 3(1A)) of the Building Regulations 2000 (as amended). This provision requires that, when windows in an existing building are replaced, the replacement work should comply with the requirements of Parts L and N. In addition, the building work once completed should not have a worse level of compliance with other applicable parts of Schedule 1 than before commencement of the work. Relevant parts of Schedule 1 may include Parts B, F and J.

3.4 To comply with Requirement F1, unless the room is ventilated adequately by other installed ventilation provisions, all replacement windows should include trickle ventilators, preferably with accessible controls as described in Table 1.5.

3.5 Alternatively, an equivalent background ventilation opening should be provided in the same room. A window with a night latch position is not normally recommended as an alternative because of the difficulty of measuring the equivalent area, the greater likelihood of draughts, and the potential increased security risk in some locations. Nevertheless a window with a night latch may be appropriate in exceptional situations where a trickle ventilator is an unsuitable solution. For example, where security considerations allow, for types of window that cannot reasonably accommodate trickle ventilators (e.g. some types of vertical sliding sash or very small windows).

3.6 In all cases, the ventilation opening should not be smaller than was originally provided, and it should be controllable. Where there was no ventilation opening, or where the size of the original ventilation opening is not known, the following minimum sizes should be adopted.

a. Dwellings:
- habitable rooms – 5000mm² equivalent area.
- kitchen, utility room and bathroom (with or without WC) – 2500mm² equivalent area.

b. Buildings other than dwellings:
- occupiable rooms: for floor areas up to 10m² – 2500mm² equivalent area; greater than 10m² at the rate of 250mm² equivalent area per m² of floor area;
- kitchens (domestic type) – 2500mm² equivalent area;
- bathrooms and shower rooms – 2500mm² equivalent area per bath or shower;
- sanitary accommodation (and/or washing facilities) – 2500mm² equivalent area per WC.

Addition of a habitable room (not including a conservatory) to an existing building

3.7 The requirements will be met by following the guidance in paragraphs 3.8 to 3.10.

3.8 The general ventilation rate for the additional room and, if necessary, adjoining rooms could be achieved by one of the following options.

a. Background ventilators could be used as follows:
  i. if the additional room is connected to an existing habitable room which now has no windows opening to outside, the guidance in paragraph 1.13 should be followed; or
  ii. if the additional room is connected to an existing habitable room which still has windows opening to outside but with a total background ventilator equivalent area less than 5000mm², the guidance in paragraph 1.13 should be followed; or
  iii. if the additional room is connected to an existing habitable room which still has windows opening to outside and with a total background ventilator equivalent area of at least 5000mm², there should be background ventilators of at least 8000mm² equivalent area between the two rooms and background ventilators of at least 8000mm² equivalent area between the additional room and outside.

b. A single room heat recovery ventilator could be used to ventilate the additional habitable room. The supply rate to that room should be determined as follows. First, determine the whole building ventilation rate from Table 1.1b. Second, calculate the room supply rate required from: (whole building ventilation rate x room volume) / (total volume of all habitable rooms).

3.9 For purge ventilation, follow the guidance in Table 1.3.

3.10 Guidance on location, controls and performance standards is given in Tables 1.4 to 1.6 respectively.

Addition of a wet room to an existing building

3.11 The requirements for the additional wet room will be met by following the guidance in paragraphs 3.12 to 3.15.

3.12 Whole building and extract ventilation can be provided by:

a. intermittent extract, as given in Table 1.2a, and a background ventilator of at least 2500mm^2 equivalent area; or

b. single room heat recovery ventilator, as given in Table 1.2a; or

c. passive stack ventilator, as given in Table 1.2b; or

d. continuous extract fan, as given in Table 1.2c.

3.13 In addition, there should be an undercut of minimum area 7600mm^2 in any internal doors, between the wet room and the existing building (equivalent to an undercut of 10mm above the floor finish for a standard 760mm width door).

3.14 For purge ventilation, follow the guidance in Table 1.3.

3.15 Guidance on location, controls and performance standards is given in Tables 1.4 to 1.6 respectively.

Addition of a conservatory to an existing building

3.16 The guidance applies to conservatories with a floor area over 30m^2.

3.17 The requirements will be met by following the guidance in paragraphs 3.18 to 3.20.

3.18 The general ventilation rate for the conservatory and, if necessary, adjoining rooms could be achieved by the use of background ventilators. Follow the guidance in paragraph 1.14 whatever the ventilation provisions in the existing room adjacent to the conservatory.

3.19 For purge ventilation, follow the guidance in Table 1.3.

3.20 Guidance on location, controls and performance standards is given in Tables 1.4 to 1.6 respectively.

Historic buildings

3.21 Conserving the special characteristics of historic buildings needs to be recognised: see BS 7913. In such work, the aim should be to improve ventilation to the extent that is necessary, taking into account the need not to prejudice the character of the historic building nor to increase the risk of long-term deterioration to the building fabric or fittings. It may be that the fabric of the historic building is more leaky than a modern building, and this can be established by pressure testing. In arriving at a balance between historic building conservation and ventilation, it would be appropriate to take into account the advice of the local planning authority's conservation officer.

3.22 Particular issues relating to work in historic buildings that warrant sympathetic treatment and where advice from others could therefore be beneficial include:

a. restoring the historic character of a building that had been subject to previous inappropriate alteration, e.g. replacement windows, doors and roof-lights;

b. rebuilding a former historic building (e.g. following a fire or filling in a gap site in a terrace);

c. making provisions enabling the fabric to 'breathe' to control moisture and potential long term decay problems: see SPAB Information Sheet No. 4, *The need for old buildings to breathe*, 1987.

Section 4: Standards and publications

Standards referred to

BS EN 378-3:2000
Refrigerating systems and heat pumps – safety and environmental requirements. Installation site and personal protection. AMD 14931 2004.

BSI PD CR 1752:1999
Ventilation for buildings – design criteria for the indoor environment.

BS 5502
Buildings and structures for agriculture. Various relevant parts including:
BS 550–33:1991 Guide to the control of odour pollution. AMD 10014 1998.
BS 550–52:1991 Code of practice for design of alarm systems, emergency ventilation and smoke ventilation for livestock housing. AMD 10014 1998.

BS 5454:2000
Recommendations for the storage and exhibition of archival documents.

BS 5925:1991
Code of practice for ventilation principles and designing for natural ventilation. AMD 8930 1995.

BS 7913:1998
Principles of the conservation of historic buildings.

BS EN 13141-1:2004
Ventilation for buildings. Performance testing of components/products for residential ventilation. Externally and internally mounted air transfer devices.

BS EN 13141-3:2004
Ventilation for buildings. Performance testing of components/products for residential ventilation. Range hoods for residential use.

BS EN 13141-4:2004
Ventilation for buildings. Performance testing of components/products for residential ventilation. Fans used in residential ventilation systems.

BS EN 13141-6:2004
Ventilation for buildings. Performance testing of components/products for residential ventilation. Exhaust ventilation system packages used in a single dwelling.

BS EN 13141-7:2004
Ventilation for buildings. Performance testing of components/products for residential ventilation. Performance testing of a mechanical supply and exhaust ventilation units (including heat recovery) for mechanical ventilation systems intended for single family dwellings.

prEN 13141-8:2004
Ventilation for buildings. Performance testing of components/products for residential ventilation. Performance testing of unducted mechanical supply and exhaust ventilation units [including heat recovery] for mechanical ventilation systems intended for a single room.

BS EN 13986:2004
Wood-based panels for use in construction. Characteristics, evaluation of conformity and marking.

Other publications referred to

American Conference of Government industrial hygienists (ACGIH)

Industrial ventilation 24th Edition, Manual of recommended practice. Available from www.acgih.org/store

Building Research Establishment (BRE)

BRE Digest 464, Part 1: *VOC emissions from building products. Sources, testing and emission data*, 2002. ISBN 1 86081 546 4

BRE Digest 464, Part 2: *VOC emissions from building products. Control, evaluation and labelling schemes*, 2002. ISBN 1 86081 547 2

BRE Report BR 417: *Building regulation health and safety*, 2001. ISBN 1 86081 475 1

Chartered Institution of Building Services Engineers (CIBSE)

Applications Manual AM10: *Natural ventilation in non-domestic buildings*, 2005. ISBN 1 80328 756 1

Applications Manual AM13: *Mixed mode ventilation*, 2000. ISBN 1 90328 701 4

CIBSE Guide A: *Environmental design*, 1999. ISBN 0 90095 396 9

CIBSE Guide B2: *Ventilation and air conditioning*, 2001. ISBN 1 90327 816 2

TM13: *Minimising the risk of Legionnaires' disease*, 2002. ISBN 1 90328 723 5

Ventilation hygiene toolkit:
BSRIA Facilities Management Specification 1 *Guidance to the standard specification for ventilation hygiene*, 2002. ISBN 0 86022 454 6
CIBSE TM26 *Hygienic maintenance of office ventilation ductwork*, 2000. ISBN 1 90328 711 1
HSE HSG 202 *General ventilation in the workplace. Guidance for employers*, 2000. ISBN 0 71761 793 9
HVCA TR17 *Guide to good practice cleanliness of ventilation systems*, 2002. ISBN 0 90378 335 5
(Withdrawn and superseded by TR/19 *Guide to good practice. Internal cleanliness of ventilation systems*, 2005. ISBN 0 90378 335 5.)

Defence Estates

Defence Works Functional Standard, Design and Maintenance Guide 08: *Space requirements for plant access operation and maintenance*, 1996. ISBN 0 11772 785 7. Available from www.defence-estates.mod.uk/publications/dmg/dmg_08.pdf

Department for Constitutional Affairs (DCA)

Court standards and design guide, 2004. CD available from the DCA

Department for Education and Skills (DfES)

Building Bulletin 101, *Ventilation of school buildings*, 2005. ISBN 0 11271 164 2. See www.teachernet.gov.uk/iaq

Department of Health Estates and Facilities Division

HTM 03; Part 1 – *Ventilation in healthcare premises: Design and validation*, 2005.

HTM 03; Part 2 – *Ventilation in healthcare premises: Verification and operational Management*, 2005.

HBN (various).

Energy Saving Trust

Good Practice Guide 192. *Designing energy efficient multi-residential buildings*, 1997. Available from www.est.org.uk/bestpractice/index.cfm.

Health and Safety Executive (HSE)

HSE Catering Information Sheet No 10, *Ventilation of kitchens in catering establishments*, 2000. Available from www.hsebooks.com.

HSE Catering Information Sheet No 11, *The main health and safety law applicable to catering*, 2000. Available from www.hsebooks.com.

HSG 37. *Introduction to local exhaust ventilation*, 1993. ISBN 0 11882 134 2

HSG 54. *Maintenance, examination and testing of local exhaust ventilation*, 1998. ISBN 0 71761 485 9

HSG 193. COSHH Essentials. Accessed on www.coshh-essentials.org.uk.

HSG 202 *General ventilation in the workplace – Guidance for employers*, 2000. ISBN 0 71761 793 9

L8 *Legionnaires' Disease: The control of legionella bacteria in water systems*. Approved code of practice and guidance, 2000. ISBN 0 71761 772 6

L24 *Workplace (Health, Safety and Welfare) Regulations 1992. Approved code of practice and guidance*, 1998. ISBN 0 71760 413 6

Legislation

Factories Act 1961, Chapter 34.

Welfare of Farm Animals (England) Regulations 2000, SI 2000/1870.

Welfare of Farm Animals (England) (Amendment) Regulations 2002, SI 2002/1646.

Welfare of Farm Animals (England) (Amendment) Regulations 2003, SI 2003/299.

Department of the Environment, Transport and the Regions (DETR)

Planning Policy Guidance (PPG) 15: *Planning and the historic environment*. Available from www.odpm.gov.uk

Society for the Protection of Ancient Buildings (SPAB)

Information Sheet No. 4, *The need for old buildings to 'breathe'*, 1987.

Glossary

For the purposes of this Approved Document the following definitions apply.

Air permeability: the physical parameter used to quantify the *air tightness* of the building fabric. It measures the resistance of the building envelope to *infiltration*. It is defined as the average volume of air (in cubic metres per hour) that passes through 1 unit area of the building envelope (in square metres) when subject to an internal to external pressure difference of 50 Pascals. The envelope area of the building is defined as the total area of the floor, walls and roof separating the interior volume from the outside environment. It is measured with ventilators closed.

Air tightness: a general descriptive term for the resistance of the building envelope to *infiltration* with ventilators closed. The greater the air tightness at a given pressure difference across the envelope, the lower the *infiltration*.

Automatic control: where a *ventilation* device is opened and closed or switched on and off or its performance is adjusted by a mechanical or electronic controller which responds to a relevant stimulus. That stimulus is usually related to the humidity of the air in a room, pollutant levels (e.g. carbon dioxide concentration in a room), occupancy of the space (e.g. using a passive infra-red motion detector) or pressure difference across the device (e.g. due to the wind outside).

Background ventilator: a small *ventilation opening* designed to provide controllable *whole building ventilation*. See Diagram 5.

Basement for dwellings: a dwelling, or a usable part of a dwelling (i.e. a habitable room), that is situated partly or entirely below ground level. Note that a cellar is distinct from a basement in that it is used only for storage, heating plant or for purposes other than habitation.

Bathroom: a room containing a bath or shower and, in addition, can also include *sanitary accommodation*.

Cellar: see *basement for dwellings*.

Closable: a *ventilation opening* which may be opened and closed under either *manual* or *automatic control*.

Common spaces: those spaces where large numbers of people are expected to gather, such as shopping malls or cinema/theatre foyers. For the purposes of this Approved Document, spaces used solely or principally for circulation (e.g. corridors and lift lobbies in office buildings and blocks of flats) are not common spaces.

Continuous operation: a mechanical ventilation device that runs all the time, e.g. mechanical extract ventilation (MEV) and mechanical ventilation with heat recovery (MVHR). The airflow rate provided by the mechanical ventilation need not be constant but may be varied, under either *manual* or *automatic control*, in response to the demand for pollutant or water vapour removal.

Equivalent area: a measure of the aerodynamic performance of a ventilator. It is the area of a sharp-edged orifice which air would pass at the same volume flow rate, under an identical applied pressure difference, as the opening under consideration.

Extract ventilation: the removal of air directly from a space or spaces to outside. Extract ventilation may be by natural means (e.g. by passive stack ventilation) or by mechanical means (e.g. by an extract fan or central system).

Free area: the geometric open area of a ventilator.

Gross internal volume: the total internal volume of the heated space, including the volume of all furniture, internal walls, internal floors, etc.

Habitable room: a room used for dwelling purposes but which is not solely a kitchen, utility room, bathroom, cellar or sanitary accommodation.

Historic building: these include: (a) listed buildings; (b) buildings situated in conservation areas; (c) buildings which are of architectural and historical interest and which are referred to as a material consideration in a local authority's development plan; (d) buildings of architectural and historical interest within national parks, areas of outstanding natural beauty and world heritage sites; and vernacular buildings of traditional form and construction.

Infiltration: the uncontrolled exchange of air between inside a building and outside through cracks, porosity and other unintentional openings in a building, caused by pressure difference effects of the wind and/or *stack effect*.

Intermittent operation: a mechanical ventilator that does not run all the time, usually only running when there is a particular need to remove pollutants or water vapour (e.g. during cooking or bathing). Intermittent operation may be under either *manual control* or *automatic control*.

Manual control: a *ventilation* device that is opened and closed or switched on and off or its performance is adjusted by the occupants of a room or building (c.f. *automatic control*).

Occupiable room: a room in a building other than a dwelling that is occupied by people, such as an office, workroom, classroom, hotel bedroom, but not a bathroom, sanitary accommodation, utility room or rooms or spaces used solely or principally for circulation, building services plant or storage purposes.

Passive stack ventilation (PSV): a ventilation device using ducts from terminals in the ceiling of rooms to terminals on the roof that extract air to outside by a combination of the natural stack effect and the pressure effects of wind passing over the roof of the building.

Permanent: a *ventilation opening* which is permanently fixed in the open position.

Purge ventilation: *manually controlled ventilation* of rooms or spaces at a relatively high rate to rapidly dilute pollutants and/or water vapour. Purge ventilation may be provided by natural means (e.g. an openable window) or by mechanical means (e.g. a fan).

Purpose-provided ventilation: that part of the *ventilation* of a building provided by ventilation devices designed into the building (e.g. via *background ventilators*, *PSV*, extract fans, mechanical ventilation or air conditioning systems).

Sanitary accommodation: a space containing one or more water closets or urinals. Sanitary accommodation containing one or more cubicles counts as a single space if there is free circulation of air throughout the space.

Stack effect: the pressure differential between inside and outside a building caused by differences in the density of the air due to an indoor/outdoor temperature difference.

Utility room: a room containing a sink or other feature or equipment which may reasonably be expected to produce water vapour in significant quantities.

Ventilation: the supply and removal of air (by natural and/or mechanical means) to and from a space or spaces in a building. It normally comprises a combination of *purpose-provided ventilation* and *infiltration*.

Ventilation opening: any means of *purpose-provided ventilation* (whether it is *permanent* or *closable*) which opens directly to external air, such as the openable parts of a window, a louvre or a *background ventilator*. It also includes any door which opens directly to external air.

Wet room: a room used for domestic activities (such as cooking, clothes washing and bathing) which give rise to significant production of airborne moisture, e.g. a kitchen, utility room or bathroom. For the purposes of Part F, sanitary accommodation is also regarded as a wet room.

Whole building ventilation (also called general ventilation): nominally continuous *ventilation* of rooms or spaces at a relatively low rate to dilute and remove pollutants and water vapour not removed by operation of *extract ventilation, purge ventilation* or *infiltration*, as well as supplying outdoor air into the building.

Diagram 5 **Provisions for background ventilation**

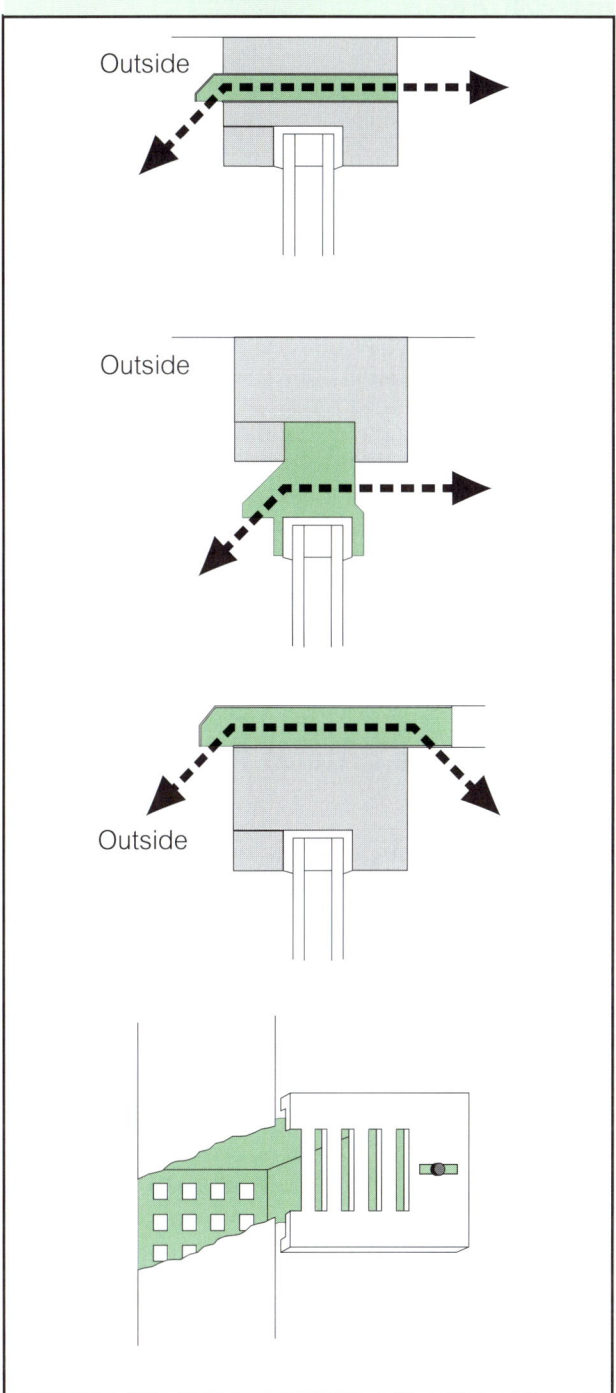

Appendix A: Performance-based ventilation

Introduction

As specified in the section on **Performance**, this Approved Document recommends ventilation provisions to control both moisture and pollutants in buildings. In order to do this, acceptable levels of moisture and other pollutants need to be defined. This Appendix sets out the levels of moisture and other pollutants that the provisions in this Approved Document are designed to control.

Note that the guidance within this Approved Document may not be adequate to address pollutants from flueless combustion space heaters or from occasional, occupant-controlled events such as painting, smoking, cleaning or other high-polluting events. It does not address the airborne spread of infection nor contamination from outdoor sources. While many of these considerations could be important factors in achieving acceptable indoor air quality, solutions are not ready for inclusion in this guidance, and indeed they may be better controlled at source (e.g. avoidance, isolation or use of lower emitting products).

Performance criteria for dwellings

The performance criterion for moisture is as follows:

- there should be no visible mould on external walls in a properly heated dwelling with typical moisture generation.

The principal performance criteria used for indoor air pollutants are as follows:

- nitrogen dioxide (NO_2) levels should not exceed:
    - 288µg/m³ (150ppb) – 1 hour average (DOH, 2004);
    - 40µg/m³ (20ppb) – long-term average (DOH, 2004);
- carbon monoxide should not exceed:
    - 100mg/m³ (90ppm) – 15 minute averaging time (DOH, 2004);
    - 60mg/m³ (50ppm) – 30 minute averaging time (DOH, 2004);
    - 30mg/m³ (25ppm) – 1 hour averaging time (DOH, 2004);
    - 10mg/m³ (10ppm) – 8 hours averaging time (DOH, 2004).
- Total volatile organic compound (TVOC) levels should not exceed 300µg/m³ averaged over 8 hours (ECA, 1992).
- Control of bio-effluents (body odours) for adapted individuals (reduction in perception due to being exposed to the environment for a period of time) will be achieved by an air supply rate of 3.5l/s/person (ASHRAE, 2003).

Assumptions used in applying performance criteria for dwellings in Section 1

General

- The dwelling has an air permeability of 3m³/h/m² at 50Pa. This is approximately equivalent to an air leakage of 3ach at 50Pa for a multi-storey dwelling and an air leakage of 4ach at 50Pa for a single-storey dwelling.

- The infiltration rate is assumed to be 1/20th of the air leakage at 50Pa (using a common 'rule-of-thumb'). This is calculated at 0.15ach for a multi-storey dwelling and 0.20ach for a single-storey dwelling. This has been applied to the ventilation system types in Tables 1.2a, 1.2b and 1.2d. As discussed in Table 1.2c, infiltration is assumed to be negligible for mechanical extract ventilation systems.

- The ventilation effectiveness is 1.0.

- For the purposes of this Approved Document, the moisture criterion will be met if the relative humidity (RH) in a room does not exceed 70% for more than 2 hours in any 12 hour period, and does not exceed 90% for more than 1 hour in any 12 hour period during the heating season.

Extract ventilation

- The principal pollutant to be removed by extract ventilation is moisture. The source rates were taken from BS 5250:2002 Table B.1.

- For intermittent extract:
    - Historically, a ventilation rate of 60l/s has been specified in the kitchen for the removal of moisture and there is no strong justification to amend it. The ventilation rate removes moisture generated at a production rate of 2000g/h. A reduced ventilation rate of 30l/s is used for a cooker hood, owing to the greater ventilation effectiveness.

    - Historically, a ventilation rate of 15l/s has been specified in the bathroom for the removal of moisture and there is no strong justification to amend it. The ventilation rate removes moisture generated at a production rate of 400g/h.

    - In the utility room, it is assumed that the ventilation rate required is 50% of that in the kitchen.

    - In WCs, the main pollutant is odour. Historically, a ventilation rate of 6l/s has been specified and there is no strong justification to amend it.

- For continuous extract:

  - In the kitchen, several scenarios were considered. Effectively, they resulted in 1000g of water vapour being released into the kitchen air at a steady rate within a 1 hour period (after allowing for absorption and migration to other rooms, etc.). The ventilation rate was selected to prevent the 70% and 90% RH limits being exceeded in the kitchen.

  - In the bathroom, several scenarios were considered. Effectively, they resulted in 650g of water vapour being released into the bathroom air at a steady rate within a 2 hour period (after allowing for absorption and migration to other rooms, etc.). The ventilation rate was selected to prevent the 70% and 90% RH limits being exceeded in the bathroom.

  - In the utility room, it was assumed that the ventilation rate required is approximately 50% of that in the kitchen. For practicality, the ventilation rate required in the bathroom has been used.

  - In WCs, the same value as intermittent extract has been applied.

  - Combustion products can be generated from cooking, particularly from the use of gas. In particular, a BRE study of UK homes has shown that the levels of nitrogen dioxide can well exceed the performance criterion (Ross and Wilde, 1999). The data from this study were analysed to determine the maximum 1 hour nitrogen dioxide level for each home. The 90th percentile value of this sample was 1155mg/m^3. Assuming a reasonable ventilation rate of 0.5ach in the kitchen during the study and an external nitrogen dioxide concentration of 20mg/m^3 to meet the performance criterion of 288mg/m^3 the extract ventilation rate in the kitchen would be required to be 2.2ach. For a kitchen of 20m^3, this equates to approximately 12l/s. Whilst this is less than required for moisture, it highlights that, if an alternative solution is determined for controlling moisture in the kitchen, 12l/s is required to adequately control the level of nitrogen dioxide. Note that, at this ventilation rate, carbon monoxide from gas cooking should also be adequately controlled.

Whole building ventilation

- The principal pollutant to be removed by whole building ventilation is moisture. The source rates were taken from BS 5250:2002 Table B.1.

- It was assumed that local extract removes 100% of the moisture generated in the bathroom and 50% of the moisture generated in the kitchen.

- An average ventilation rate was selected which removed all of the moisture produced in the dwelling over a 24 hour period (except for moisture removed by local extract). Further calculations, using typical occupant profiles (and moisture generation profiles), showed that the average relative humidity in the dwelling should not exceed 70% for more than 2 hours in any 12 hour period during winter and should not exceed 90% for more than 1 hour in any 12 hour period during winter.

- This results in the values in Table 1.1b.

- Note that these calculations are based on winter weather conditions. During warmer spring and autumn periods, the moisture removal capacity of the outdoor air will be less (i.e. the outdoor air on being heated to the internal temperature within the dwelling will have a higher relative humidity in the spring and autumn periods) and additional ventilation may be required. The provisions for purge ventilation (e.g. windows) may be used for this purpose.

- There are other pollutants which must also be adequately controlled. These are particularly important in homes of low occupant density where moisture production is low for the size of the property. Levels of volatile organic compounds were monitored in a recent BRE study of UK homes (Dimitroulopoulou et al, 2005). From these data, the total source production rate of volatile organic compounds was determined to be 300mg/h per m^2 of floor area. To meet the performance criterion of 300mg/m^3, it requires a minimum whole building ventilation rate of 0.3 l/s per m^2 internal floor area.

Purge ventilation

- A value of 4ach has been selected as:

  - it provides a purge ventilation rate an order of magnitude above whole building ventilation;

  - it is similar to the ventilation rate provided by windows in the 1995 edition of Approved Document F. The calculation assumes single-sided ventilation for a dwelling in an urban environment and an internal/ external temperature difference of 3°C.

Table 1.2 – whole building ventilation rates

- In determining the ventilation rates, the air supply rates in Table 1.1b have been used.

- The air supply rate has been reduced by 0.15ach (or 0.20ach for single-storey buildings) to allow for infiltration.

- To determine the equivalent areas, the standard airflow equation has been used as below:

$A = 1000. (Q/C_d).(\rho/2.\Delta P)^{0.5}$

Where:

A = the background ventilator equivalent area (mm^2)

Q = the air supply rate (l/s)

C_d = the discharge coefficient, taken as 0.61

ρ = the air density (kg/m3), taken as 1.2

ΔP = the pressure across the vent, which has been taken as 0.6Pa for single-storey dwellings and 1.0Pa for multi-storey dwellings.

Note that the total actual equivalent area required (A_T) is double that derived from the equation above. This only provides the equivalent area for air supplied to the dwelling. A similar equivalent area is required for air to exit the dwelling.

Note that in determining these pressure differences, a meteorological wind speed of 4m/s at 10m height was taken (based on BS 5925:1991) and an internal/external temperature difference of 15°C.

Performance criteria for buildings other than dwellings

The main guidance within this document has focused on offices. For this, the main criteria have been:

- A supply rate, in the absence of tobacco smoking or other excessive pollutants, of 10l/s/person, based upon surveys which indicate that below this level the incidence of health effects becomes increasingly significant. This will also satisfy the requirement of 8l/s/person needed to control bioeffluents for unadapted individuals.

- There should be no visible mould on external walls in a properly heated dwelling with typical moisture generation.

- Nitrogen dioxide (NO_2) levels should not exceed:
  - 288µg/m³ (150ppb) – 1 hour average (Department of the Environment, 1996);
  - 40µg/m³ (21ppb) – long-term average (WHO, 2003).

- Carbon monoxide for the general population should not exceed
  - 100mg/m³ (90ppm) – 15 minute averaging time (WHO, 2000);
  - 60mg/m³ (50ppm) – 30 minute averaging time (WHO, 2000);
  - 30mg/m³ (25ppm) – 1 hour averaging time (WHO, 2000);
  - 10mg/m³ (10ppm) – 8 hours averaging time (Department of the Environment, 1994a).

- Carbon monoxide for occupational exposure should not exceed:
  - 35mg/m³ (30ppm) – 8 hours averaging time (HSE, 2003).

- Total volatile organic compound (TVOC) levels should not exceed 300µg/m³ averaged over 8 hours (ECA, 1992).

- Ozone levels should not exceed 100µg/m³ (Department of the Environment, 1994b).

Note that the guidance within this Approved Document may not be adequate to address pollutants from occasional, occupant-controlled events such as painting, smoking, cleaning or other high-polluting events. While these could be important factors in achieving acceptable indoor air quality, solutions are not ready for inclusion in this guidance, and indeed they may be better controlled at source (e.g. avoidance, isolation or use of lower emitting products).

Where the Health and Safety Executive gives guidance for specific situations, it should be followed in preference to the guidance given here.

Assumptions used in applying performance criteria for offices in Section 2

General

- The office has an air permeability of 3m³/h/m² at 50Pa.

- At this level of air permeability, in large buildings (low ratio of surface area to volume contained), infiltration can be assumed to be negligible compared with the purpose-provided ventilation.

- The ventilation effectiveness is 0.9 (for Table 2.1b).

- For the purposes of this Approved Document, the moisture criterion will be met if the relative humidity in a room does not exceed 70% for more than 2 hours in any 12 hour period, and does not exceed 90% for more than 1 hour in any 12 hour period, during the heating season.

Extract ventilation

- Office equipment can emit pollutants including ozone and organic compounds. For example, a study by Black and Wortham (1999) suggests the following emission rates for laser printers and dry paper copiers assuming 30 minutes continual use in an hour:
  - 25mg/h for TVOCs;
  - 3mg/h for ozone.

To meet the performance criteria for these pollutants requires an extract rate of 20l/s per machine during use.

- For the sanitary accommodation, the extract rates used for dwellings have been applied.

- For food and beverage preparation areas, the extract rates used for dwellings have been applied.

Whole building ventilation

- A number of studies have investigated ventilation and health in offices (principally sick building syndrome). Although there is no clear threshold ventilation rate below which health suddenly worsens, a number of sources have identified 10l/s/p as a significant level. This can probably be traced back to an analysis of experimental studies of office buildings by Mendell (1993). Hence the recommendation within the Approved Document for 10l/s/p for buildings with no smoking and no significant pollutant sources.

- Increasing the ventilation rate above 10l/s/p may improve health (results unclear), but there are diminishing returns (i.e. the improvement in health per l/s/p increase in ventilation rate becomes smaller as the ventilation rate increases). It suggests that there is little advantage in increasing the whole building ventilation rate above 10l/s/p. Increased ventilation has a cost in economic and environmental terms. Having set a ventilation rate of 10l/s/p, if further improvements in indoor air quality are necessary, alternative approaches should be considered first, e.g. use of low-emission materials.

Purge ventilation

- There are normally more options for the removal of high concentrations of pollutants from office spaces than for dwellings (e.g. leaving rooms unoccupied until acceptable pollutant levels are achieved). Hence, general guidance has been provided rather than specifying any ventilation rate(s).

References

ASHRAE (2003). *Ventilation and acceptable indoor air quality in low-rise residential buildings.* ASHRAE Standard 62.2.

Black M S and Wortham A W (1999). *Emissions from office equipment.* Proceedings of the 8th International Conference on Indoor Air Quality and Climate, Indoor Air 99, Edinburgh 8–13 August 1999, Vol. 2, pp455–459.

BS 5250:2002 Code of practice for the control of condensation in buildings. BSI.

Department of the Environment (1994a). *Expert panel on air quality standards: Carbon monoxide.* London, HMSO. www.defra.gov.uk/environment/airquality/aqs

Department of the Environment (1994b). *Expert panel on air quality standards: Ozone.* London, HMSO. www.defra.gov.uk/environment/airquality/aqs

Department of the Environment (1996). *Expert panel on air quality standards: Nitrogen dioxide.* London, The Stationery Office. www.defra.gov.uk/environment/airquality/aqs

Department of Health (2004). Committee on the Medical Effects of Air Pollutants. Guidance on the effects on health of indoor air pollutants. http://www.advisorybodies.doh.gov.uk/comeap/PDFS/guidanceindoorairqualitydec04.pdf

Dimitroulopoulou C, Crump D, Coward S K D, Brown V, Squire R, Mann H, White M, Pierce B and Ross D (2005). *Ventilation, air tightness and indoor air quality in new homes.* Report BR 477. BRE bookshop.

ECA (1992). European Concerted Action on indoor air and its impact on man: Guidelines for ventilation requirements in buildings. Working Group Report No.11. EUR 14449 EN. Commission of the European Communities, Luxembourg.

HSE (2003). *Occupational exposure limits 2002, plus supplement 2003.* HSE Books.

Mendell M J (1993). *Non-specific symptoms in office workers: a review and summary of the epidemiologic literature.* Indoor air 3, 227–236.

Ross D I and Wilde D (1999). *Continuous monitoring of nitrogen dioxide and carbon monoxide levels in UK homes.* Proceedings of the 8th International Conference on Indoor Air Quality and Climate, Indoor Air 99, Edinburgh 8-13 August 1999, Vol. 3, pp147–152.

WHO (2000). *Guidelines for air quality.* World Health Organization, Geneva.

WHO (2003). *WHO working group meeting: Review of health aspects of air pollution with particulate matter, ozone and nitrogen dioxide,* Bonn, Germany, 13–15 January 2003.

Appendix B: Purge ventilation

Introduction

Adequate purge ventilation may be achieved by the use of openable windows and/or external doors. This Appendix provides details of necessary window and door sizes. It is a simplification of guidance in BS 5925:1991 Code of practice for ventilation principles and designing for natural ventilation. The diagrams below highlight the window dimensions of importance.

Windows

- For a hinged or pivot window that opens 30° or more, or for sliding sash windows, the height x width of the opening part should be at least 1/20 of the floor area of the room.

- For a hinged or pivot window that opens less than 30°, the height x width of the opening part should be at least 1/10 of the floor area of the room.

- If the room contains more than one openable window, the areas of all the opening parts may be added to achieve the required proportion of the floor area. The required proportion of the floor area is determined by the opening angle of the largest window in the room.

- Note that Approved Document B includes provisions for the size of escape windows. The larger of the provisions in Approved Document B or F should apply in all cases.

External doors (including patio doors)

- For an external door, the height x width of the opening part should be at least 1/20 of the floor area of the room.

- If the room contains more than one external door, the areas of all the opening parts may be added to achieve at least 1/20 of the floor area of the room.

- If the room contains a combination of at least one external door and at least one openable window, the areas of all the opening parts may be added to achieve at least 1/20 of the floor area of the room.

Window dimensions

Window opening area = H x W

(H and W are the dimensions of the open area)

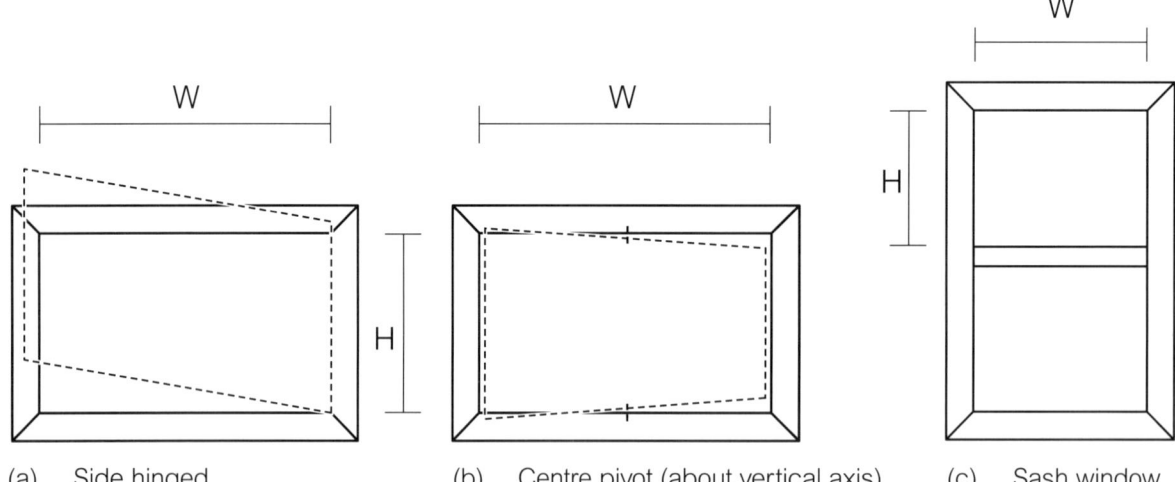

(a)　Side hinged　　　(b)　Centre pivot (about vertical axis)　　　(c)　Sash window

Appendix C: Example calculations for ventilation sizing for dwellings

Introduction

This appendix provides example calculations for each ventilation system set out in paragraph 1.8. A ground-floor flat and a semi-detached house have been considered for each system type. Thus there are eight examples as follows.

Ground-floor flat:

- Example C1 – Background ventilators and intermittent extract fans
- Example C2 – Passive stack ventilation
- Example C3 – Continuous mechanical extract
- Example C4 – Continuous mechanical supply and extract

Semi-detached house:

- Example C5 – Background ventilators and intermittent extract fans
- Example C6 – Passive stack ventilation
- Example C7 – Continuous mechanical extract
- Example C8 – Continuous mechanical supply and extract

Ground-floor flat

Description

The flat contains the following rooms:

- kitchen;
- combined living/dining room;
- one double bedroom;
- internal bathroom containing WC; and in addition
- all rooms have an external wall except for the bathroom.

The floor plan is given in Diagram C1.

Assumptions:

- cooker hood adjacent to cooker hob;
- gross internal volume of the heated space of 83m³;
- total floor area of 36m²;
- two person occupancy; and
- side-hinged windows 1.0m high and openable to 60°.

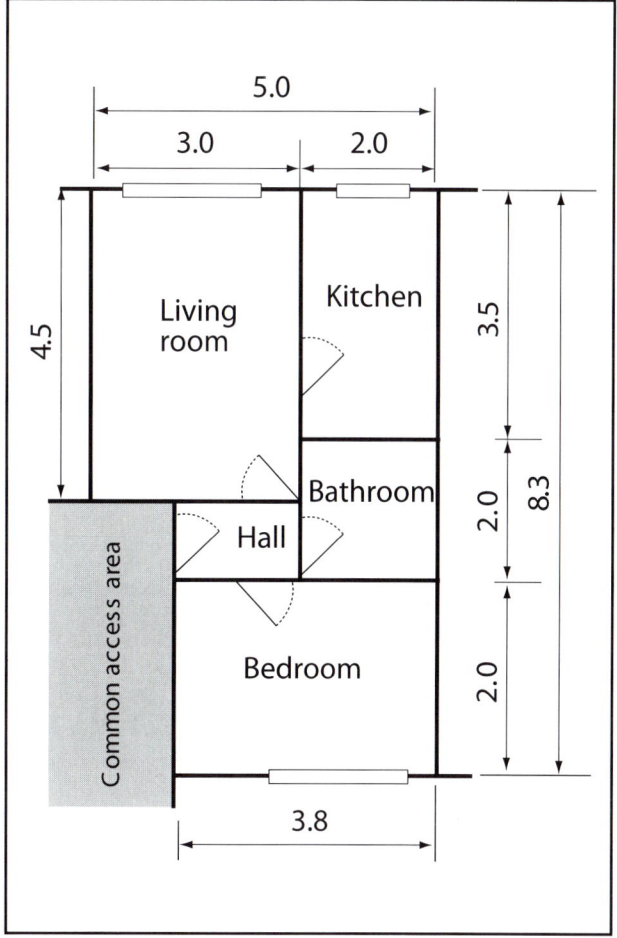

Diagram C1 **Ground-floor flat plan example**

Example C1 **Background ventilators and intermittent extract fans (this is based on Table 1.2a)**

Intermittent extract

Room	Intermittent extract rate
Kitchen	30l/s (adjacent to hob)
Bathroom	15l/s

Background ventilators

- For a single-storey ground-floor dwelling of 36m² floor area, the table shows that the equivalent background ventilator area is 30,000mm² (this includes the additional 5000mm² as we are considering a single-storey building).

- To maximise the airflow through the dwelling by encouraging cross ventilation, it is best to locate similar equivalent areas of background ventilators on opposite sides of the dwelling.

Purge ventilation

- Calculate the percentage window opening area (percentage of floor area) for each room having an external wall.

- Using Appendix B with an opening angle of 60° gives: 1/20 of the floor area.

- Therefore, for a living room of 13.5m² floor area there should be a window opening area of at least 0.68m². This calculation should be carried out for all habitable rooms.

Example C2 **Passive stack ventilation (this is based on Table 1.2b)**

Choose appropriate passive stack ventilation provision

Room	Internal duct diameter (mm)	Internal cross-sectional area (mm²)
Kitchen	125	12,000
Bathroom	100	8000

Background ventilators

Calculate the total equivalent area of ventilators required for a dwelling as follows:

- **Step 1:** for a single-storey ground-floor dwelling of 36m² floor area, Table 1.2a shows that the equivalent background ventilator area is 30,000mm² (this includes the additional 5000mm² as we are considering a single-storey building).

- **Step 2:** for a PSV in both the kitchen and bathroom, an allowance of 5000mm² can be made.

- **Step 3:** 30,000 – 5000 = 25,000mm².

- In addition, the equivalent area must be at least the total cross-sectional area of the ducts (20,000mm²), which it is. It should be distributed with similar areas on opposite sides of the dwelling (but not in the kitchen and bathroom).

Purge ventilation

- Calculate the percentage window opening area (percentage of floor area) for each room having an external wall.

- Using Appendix B with an opening angle of 60° gives: 1/20 of the floor area.

- Therefore, for a living room of 13.5m² floor area there should be a window opening area of at least 0.68m². This calculation should be carried out for all habitable rooms.

Example C3 **Continuous mechanical extract (this is based on Table 1.2c)**

Continuous extract

Step 1: Whole building ventilation rate is 13l/s.

Step 2: Whole dwelling extract rate is 21l/s (assuming extract in kitchen and bathroom).

Step 3: • Maximum rate (e.g. boost) is at least 21l/s (with a minimum of 13l/s in the kitchen and 8l/s in the bathroom).

    • The minimum rate is at least 13l/s (spread between the kitchen and bathroom).

Background ventilators

• Background ventilators of at least 2500mm^2 equivalent area should be located in the living room and bedroom.

Purge ventilation

• Calculate the percentage window opening area (percentage of floor area) for each room having an external wall.

• Using Appendix B with an opening angle of 60° gives: 1/20 of the floor area.

• Therefore, for a living room of 13.5m^2 floor area there should be a window opening area of at least 0.68m^2. This calculation should be carried out for all habitable rooms.

Example C4 **Continuous mechanical supply and extract with heat recovery (this is based on Table 1.2d)**

Continuous supply and extract

Step 1: Calculate the whole building ventilation supply rate:

    i. from the table, the air supply rate = 13l/s;

    ii. allow for infiltration by subtracting 0.06 x gross internal volume of the dwelling (m^3).

    Ventilation rate = 13 – 0.06 x 83 = 8l/s

Step 2: Calculate the whole dwelling air extract rate at maximum operation:

    whole dwelling extract rate for the dwelling is 21l/s (assuming extract in kitchen and bathroom).

Step 3: • Maximum rate (e.g. boost) is at least 21l/s (with 13l/s extract in the kitchen and 8l/s extract in the bathroom).

    • The minimum rate is at least 8l/s.

Purge ventilation

• Calculate the percentage window opening area (percentage of floor area) for each room having an external wall.

• Using Appendix B with an opening angle of 60° gives: 1/20 of the floor area.

• Therefore, for a living room of 13.5m^2 floor area there should be a window opening area of at least 0.68m^2. This calculation should be carried out for all habitable rooms.

Semi-detached house

Description

The semi-detached house contains the following rooms:

- entrance hall/stairway;
- kitchen;
- dining room;
- living room;
- three bedrooms;
- bathroom containing WC; and in addition
- all rooms have an external wall.

The floor plan is given in Diagrams C2 and C3.

Assumptions:

- cooker hood adjacent to cooker hob;
- gross internal volume of the heated space of 210m³;
- total floor area of 84m²;
- four person occupancy; and
- side-hinged windows 1.0m high and openable to a fixed position of 15º.

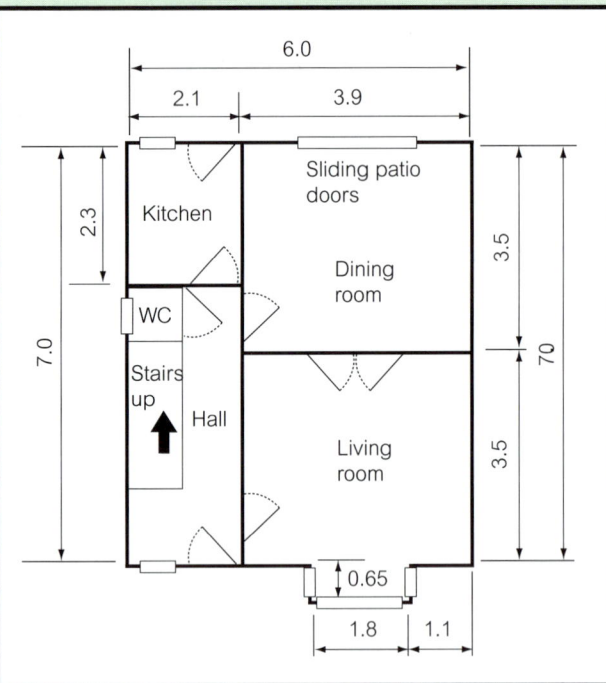

Diagram C2 **Semi-detached house ground-floor plan example**

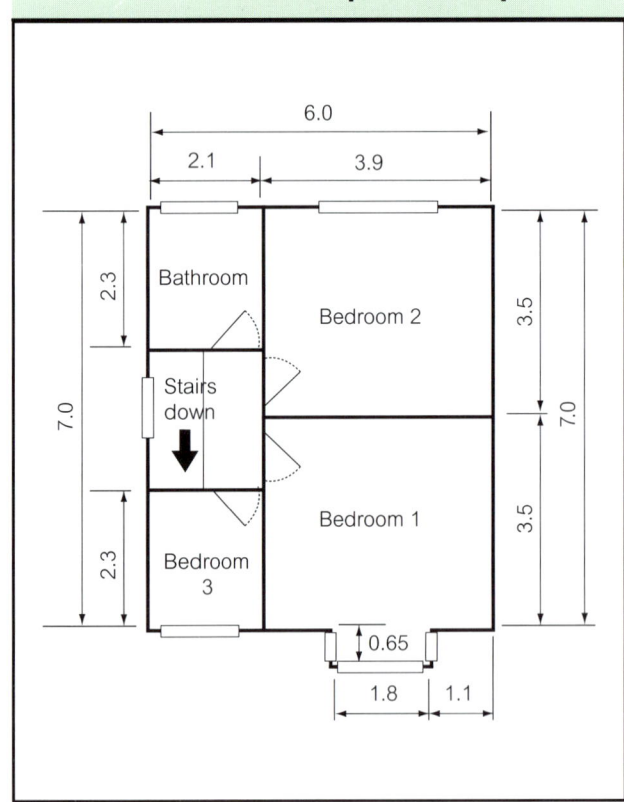

Diagram C3 **Semi-detached house first-floor plan example**

Example C5 **Background ventilators and intermittent extract fans (this is based on Table 1.2a)**

Intermittent extract

Room	Intermittent extract rate
Kitchen	30l/s (adjacent to hob)
Bathroom	15l/s

Background ventilators

- For a two-storey semi-detached house of 84m^2 floor area, the table shows that the equivalent background ventilator area is 40,000mm^2.

- To maximise the airflow through the dwelling by encouraging cross ventilation, it is best to locate similar equivalent areas of background ventilators on opposite sides of the dwelling.

Purge ventilation

- Calculate the percentage window opening area (percentage of floor area) for each room having an external wall.

- Using Appendix B with an opening angle of 15° gives: 1/10 of the floor area.

- Therefore, for a living room of 14.8m^2 floor area there should be a window opening area of at least 1.48m^2. This calculation should be carried out for all habitable rooms.

Example C6 **Passive stack ventilation (this is based on Table 1.2b)**

Choose appropriate passive stack ventilation provision

Room	Internal duct diameter (mm)	Internal cross-sectional area (mm^2)
Kitchen	125	12,000
Bathroom	100	8000

Background ventilators

Calculate the total equivalent area of ventilators required for a dwelling as follows:

- **Step 1:** for a two-storey semi-detached house of 84m^2 floor area, Table 1.2a shows that the equivalent background ventilator area is 40,000mm^2.

- **Step 2:** for a PSV in both the kitchen and bathroom, an allowance of 5000mm^2 can be made.

- **Step 3:** 40,000 – 5000 = 35,000mm^2.

- In addition, the equivalent area must be at least the total cross-sectional area of the ducts (20,000mm^2), which it is. It should be distributed with similar areas on opposite sides of the dwelling (but not in the kitchen and bathroom).

Purge ventilation

- Calculate the percentage window opening area (percentage of floor area) for each room having an external wall.

- Using Appendix B with an opening angle of 15° gives: 1/10 of the floor area.

- Therefore, for a living room of 14.8m^2 floor area there should be a window opening area of at least 1.48m^2. This calculation should be carried out for all habitable rooms.

Example C7 **Continuous mechanical extract (this is based on Table 1.2c)**

Continuous extract

Step 1: • Whole building ventilation rate from the list in the table is 21l/s.

• However, minimum air supply rate = 0.3 x floor area = 0.3 x 84 = 25l/s.

• Hence, whole house air supply rate is 25l/s.

Step 2: Whole dwelling extract rate is 21l/s (assuming extract in kitchen and bathroom).

Step 3: • In this case the required whole house supply rate is greater than the whole house extract rate, and only a minimum extract rate of 25l/s is required (with at least 13l/s in the kitchen and 8l/s in the bathroom).

Background ventilators

• Background ventilators of at least 2500mm² equivalent area should be located in the living room, dining room and each bedroom.

Purge ventilation

• Calculate the percentage window opening area (percentage of floor area) for each room having an external wall.

• Using Appendix B with an opening angle of 15° gives: 1/10 of the floor area.

• Therefore, for a living room of 14.8m² floor area there should be a window opening area of at least 1.48m². This calculation should be carried out for all habitable rooms.

Example C8 **Continuous mechanical supply and extract with heat recovery (this is based on Table 1.2d)**

Continuous supply and extract

Step 1: Calculate the whole dwelling air supply rate:

i.   Whole building ventilation rate for the dwelling from the list in the table is 21l/s.

However, minimum air supply rate = 0.3 x floor area = 0.3 x 84 = 25l/s.

Hence, whole dwelling air supply rate is 25l/s.

ii. Allow for infiltration by subtracting 0.04 x gross internal volume of the dwelling (m³):

Ventilation rate = 25 – 0.04 x 210 = 17l/s.

Step 2: Calculate the whole dwelling air extract rate at maximum operation:

whole dwelling extract rate is 21l/s (assuming extract in kitchen and bathroom).

Step 3: • Maximum rate (e.g. boost) is at least 21l/s (with 13l/s extract in the kitchen and 8l/s extract in the bathroom).

• The minimum rate is at least 17l/s.

Purge ventilation

• Calculate the percentage window opening area (percentage of floor area) for each room having an external wall.

• Using Appendix B with an opening angle of 15° gives: 1/10 of the floor area.

• Therefore, for a living room of 14.8m² floor area there should be a window opening area of at least 1.48m². This calculation should be carried out for all habitable rooms.

Appendix D: Passive stack ventilation system design and installation guidance

The design and installation of passive stack ventilation systems (PSV) can have a significant influence on their performance. However, if the following guidance is closely followed adequate performance may be assumed to have been achieved.

Design – system layout

- The layouts shown in Diagram D1 are considered to be suitable for the majority of dwellings of up to four storeys. Placing the outlet terminal at the ridge of the roof (Diagram D1(a)) is the preferred option for reducing the adverse effects of wind gusts and certain wind directions. A tile ventilator may be used to terminate a PSV system on the roof slope but the terminal must be positioned no more than 0.5m from the roof ridge. If the duct penetrates the roof more than 0.5m from the ridge, it must extend above the roof slope to at least ridge height to ensure that the duct terminal is in the negative pressure region above the roof (Diagram D1(b)).

- Separate ducts are taken from the ceilings of the kitchen, bathroom, utility room or WC to separate terminals on the roof. Do not use common outlet terminals or branched ducts.

- Ducts should ideally use no more than one offset (i.e. no more than two bends) and these should be of the 'swept' rather than 'sharp' type to minimise flow resistance. Offsets at an angle of no more than 45° to the vertical are preferred (Diagram D2).

- If a dwelling in which PSV is proposed is situated near a significantly taller building (i.e. more than 50% taller), it should be at least five times the difference in height away from the taller building (e.g. if the difference in height is 10m, PSV should not be installed in a dwelling within 50m of the taller building).

Diagram D1 **Suitable layouts for PSV systems**

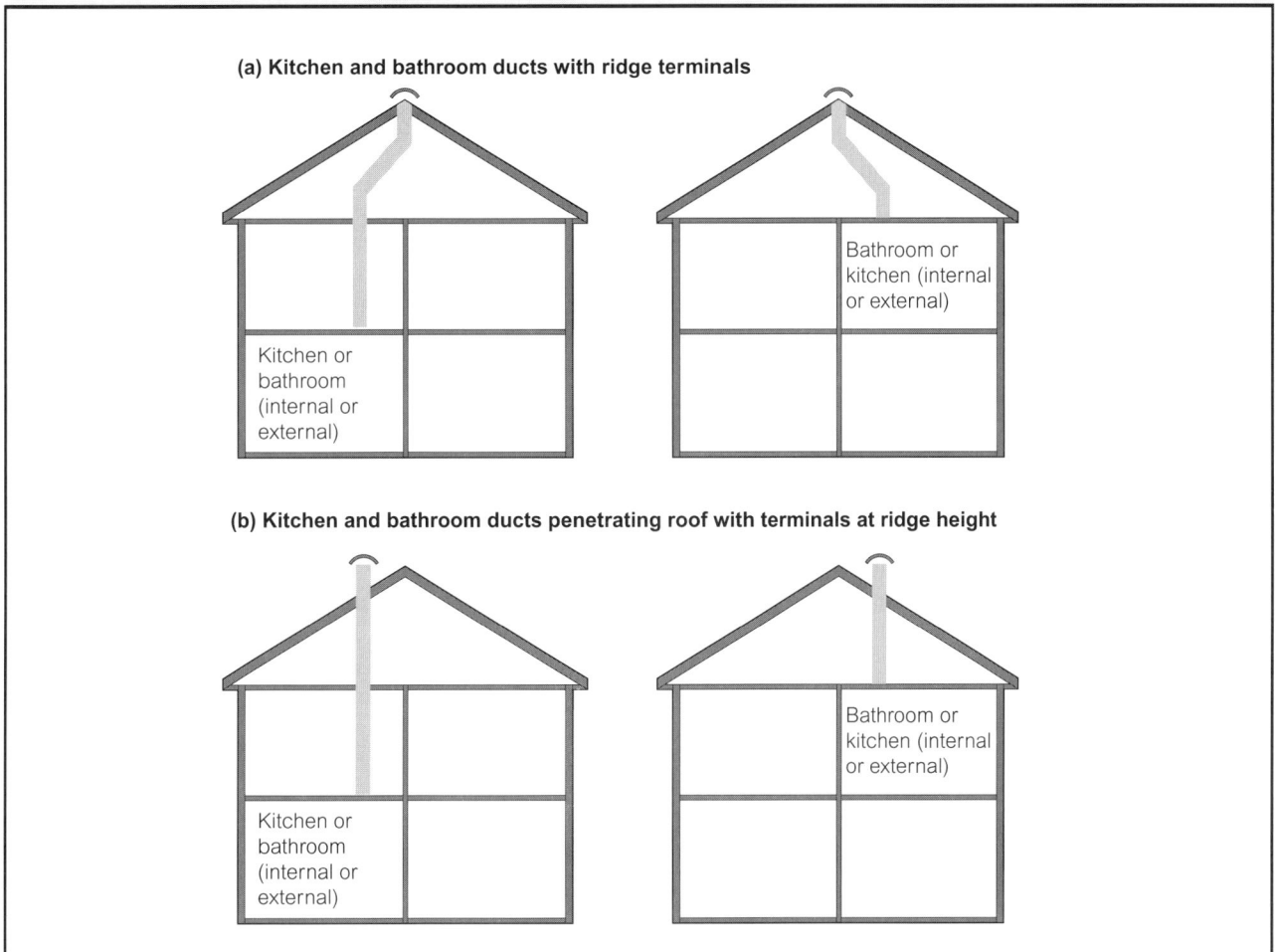

(a) Kitchen and bathroom ducts with ridge terminals

Kitchen or bathroom (internal or external)

Bathroom or kitchen (internal or external)

(b) Kitchen and bathroom ducts penetrating roof with terminals at ridge height

Kitchen or bathroom (internal or external)

Bathroom or kitchen (internal or external)

Diagram D2 **Suitable and unsuitable bends for passive stack ducts**

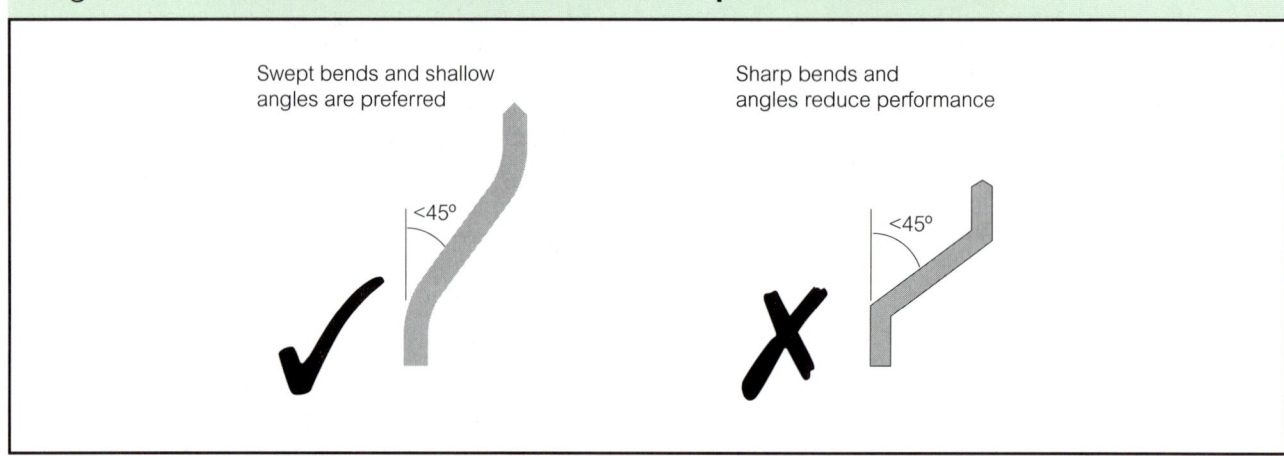

Swept bends and shallow angles are preferred

Sharp bends and angles reduce performance

Design – component specifications

- Ceiling extract grilles should have a free area of not less than the duct cross-sectional area (when in the fully open position if adjustable).

- Both rigid ducting (e.g. PVCu pipes and fittings) and flexible ducting are suitable for PSV systems and have similar resistance to airflow at typical PSV system airflow rates.

- Ducts should be insulated in the roof space and other unheated areas with at least 25mm of a material having a thermal conductivity of 0.04W/m·K. Where a duct extends above roof level the section above the roof should be insulated or a condensation trap should be fitted just below roof level.

- The outlet terminal should have a free area of not less than the duct cross-sectional area. If a conversion fitting is required to connect the duct to the terminal then the duct cross-sectional area must be maintained (or exceeded) throughout the conversion fitting so as not to restrict the flow. The terminal should not allow ingress of large insects or birds and should be designed so that rain is not likely to enter the duct and run down into the dwelling. The terminal should also be designed such that any condensation forming inside it cannot run down into the dwelling but will run off onto the roof.

- Roof terminal design can be critical to PSV system performance. As a general guide, gas flue terminals tested to BS 715:1993 and having the required free areas are likely to perform well aerodynamically but may suffer from excessive water penetration in heavy or driving rain conditions. Specially made PSV roof outlet terminals should also perform well aerodynamically and are generally designed to resist water penetration to a greater extent than gas flue terminals. A draft European Standard for testing cowls and roof outlets is in preparation (prEN 13141-5) but at present there is insufficient information to recommend

specific minimum or maximum values for performance parameters derived from that Standard. As interim guidance it is suggested that terminals, with any necessary conversion fitting, should have an overall static pressure loss (upstream duct static minus test room static) equivalent to no more than four times the mean duct velocity pressure when measured at a static pressure difference of 10 Pascal.

Installation

- Carefully measure the length of duct to be used such that it is just sufficient to fit between the ceiling grille and the outlet terminal. Flexible ducting should be fully extended but not taut, allowing approximately 300mm extra to make smooth bends in an offset system.

- Ducting should be properly supported along its length to ensure that the duct can run straight without distortion or sagging and that there are no kinks at any bends or the connections to ceiling grilles and outlet terminals. Flexible ducting generally requires more support than rigid ducting.

- In the roof space it is recommended that the duct be secured to a wooden strut that is securely fixed at both ends. A flexible duct should be allowed to curve gently at each end of the strut to attach to the ceiling grille and roof outlet terminal.

- Use a rigid duct for that part of a PSV system which is outside, above the roof slope, to give it stability. It should project down into the roof space far enough to allow firm support.

- Ensure that the duct is securely fixed to the roof outlet terminal so that it cannot sag or become detached.

Operation of PSV in hot weather

A PSV unit should extract sufficient air from the wet rooms during the heating season. However, during warmer weather, particularly the summer months, the temperature difference between the internal and external air will be significantly reduced. Consequently, the stack driving pressures will be reduced and, to ensure adequate ventilation during the warmer months, provision for purge ventilation should also be made in these wet rooms.

Fire precautions

Where a dwelling extends to three or more storeys, and in blocks of flats, fire precautions may be required to ensure that escape routes are not prejudiced by the presence of PSV ducts. Guidance on such fire precautions may be found in Building Regulations: Approved Document B.

Noise

In locations where external noise is likely to be intrusive (e.g. near busy roads and airports) some sound attenuation in the duct is desirable. In such situations it is suggested that fitting a proprietary sound attenuator duct section in the roof space just above the ceiling is likely to be effective.

Appendix E: Good practice guide to the installation of fans for dwellings

Introduction

The following is offered as general guidance, but accurate system design using manufacturers' performance data is recommended. In such designs, the resistance of the ducted system should be matched against the selected fan performance curve (available from the manufacturer) to achieve the installed performance for the room type referred to in the Approved Document.

With all installations it is important that simple good practice is followed to ensure that the fan installed is capable of meeting the relevant requirements. Different fan types should be used for the applications they are designed to meet. If the wrong fan type is used there is a risk of it not performing to the required airflow rate and also a chance of reducing its operational life.

This document covers four main fan types commonly used in domestic applications:

1. axial fans – wall or window and short ducts through the ceiling;
2. centrifugal – wall or window for exposed sites and longer ducts through the ceiling;
3. in-line axial fans for ducted applications;
4. in-line mixed flow fans.

If an application falls outside the limits described within this Appendix then alternative methods, such as those described elsewhere in this Approved Document, should be considered.

Axial fans

The axial fan is the most common form of fan used for wall and window mounting applications. A short length of rigid round duct at least the same diameter as the fan outlet or equally sized flexible duct pulled taut is suitable to duct them through a wall up to 350mm thick.

Where necessary, the manufacturer may supply a window kit allowing the fan to be installed through a suitable glazing hole.

Bathroom applications using 100mm diameter fans can also utilise an axial fan for installations in the ceiling with up to 1.5m of flexible duct and two 90° bends. The duct must be pulled taut and the discharge terminal should have at least 85% free area of the duct diameter. Normally, any extension of the duct beyond this length will cause performance to drop. However, manufacturers' data should be referred to.

Centrifugal fans

Centrifugal fans develop greater pressure allowing longer lengths of ducting to be used. They may also be used for wall or window applications in high rise (above three storeys) or exposed locations to overcome wind pressure.

Centrifugal fans are mostly designed with 100mm diameter outlets, which enable them to be connected to a wide variety of duct types. However, good practice still applies as detailed in the general notes section at the end of this Appendix.

In general:

*   If using a wall/ceiling mounted centrifugal fan designed to achieve 60l/s for kitchens with 100mm diameter flexible duct or rectangular ducting it should not be ducted further than 3m with 1 x 90° bend.
*   If using a wall/ceiling mounted centrifugal fan designed to achieve 15l/s for bathrooms with 100mm diameter flexible duct or rectangular ducting it should not be ducted further than 6m with 2 x 90° bends.

Note: Where this is not practical, a trade-off may be permitted such that the addition of one bend will equate to a reduction of 1m in duct length.

It should be noted that recirculating cooker hoods do not fulfil the ventilation requirements of Part F.

In-line fans

The in-line fan type of installation has some advantages to offer over that of a typical window/wall fan installation, but there is a trade-off to be made. These systems are generally available for bathrooms (100mm diameter), utility rooms (125mm diameter) and kitchens (150mm diameter).

In-line axial fan

An in-line axial fan should be installed with the shortest possible duct length to the discharge terminal. Refer to manufacturers' data.

In-line mixed flow fans

An in-line mixed flow inline fan is a hybrid with the mixed characteristics of axial fans and centrifugal fans allowing them to be used on longer lengths of ducting. Refer to manufacturers' data.

Terminals

For this situation only, the equivalent area may be assumed to be equal to the free area.

1. Room Terminal: Extract grille
Ensure that the equivalent area of the grille opening is a minimum of 85% of the equivalent area of the ducting being used.

2. Discharge Terminal
Ensure that the equivalent area of the grille opening is a minimum of 85% of the equivalent area of the ducting being used.

General notes

- Adequate replacement air must also be available, e.g. a 10mm gap under the door or equivalent.

- Fans and ducting placed in or passing through unheated voids or loft spaces should be insulated to reduce the possibility of condensation forming.

- Where a duct rises vertically it may be necessary to fit a condensation trap in order to prevent backflow of any moisture into the product.

- Horizontal ducting, including ducting in walls, should be arranged to slope slightly downwards away from the fan to prevent backflow of any moisture into the product.

- All duct runs should be straight, with as few bends and kinks as possible to minimise system resistance.

- Where ducting passes through a fire-stopping wall or fire compartment, the required measures to ensure compliance with Part B of the Building Regulations must be taken.

- All flexible ducting should be pulled taut to minimise system resistance.

- The inner radius of any bend should be greater or equal to the diameter of the ducting being used. If the radius is reduced, the resistance of the bend will increase and the volume of air being extracted will decrease (see Diagram E1).

- To reduce any incidence of draught it is desirable that a device (back-draught) be introduced into the system, this may be incorporated into the fan itself.

- Rectangular ducting is also available. Its use should fall within the limitations of the duct length guidelines given in this Appendix.

- Care should be taken when positioning the ducting to ensure that it cannot be damaged through occupier use of the space in which it is installed.

- Ensure flexible ducting is installed without peaks or troughs (see Diagram E1a).

- Ensure that the circular profile of flexible duct is maintained throughout the full length of the duct run. Where the flexible ducting passes through a smaller gap and the flexible duct is deformed, the resistance will increase, leading to loss of extracted air volume (see Diagram E1b).

Diagram E1 **Correct installation**

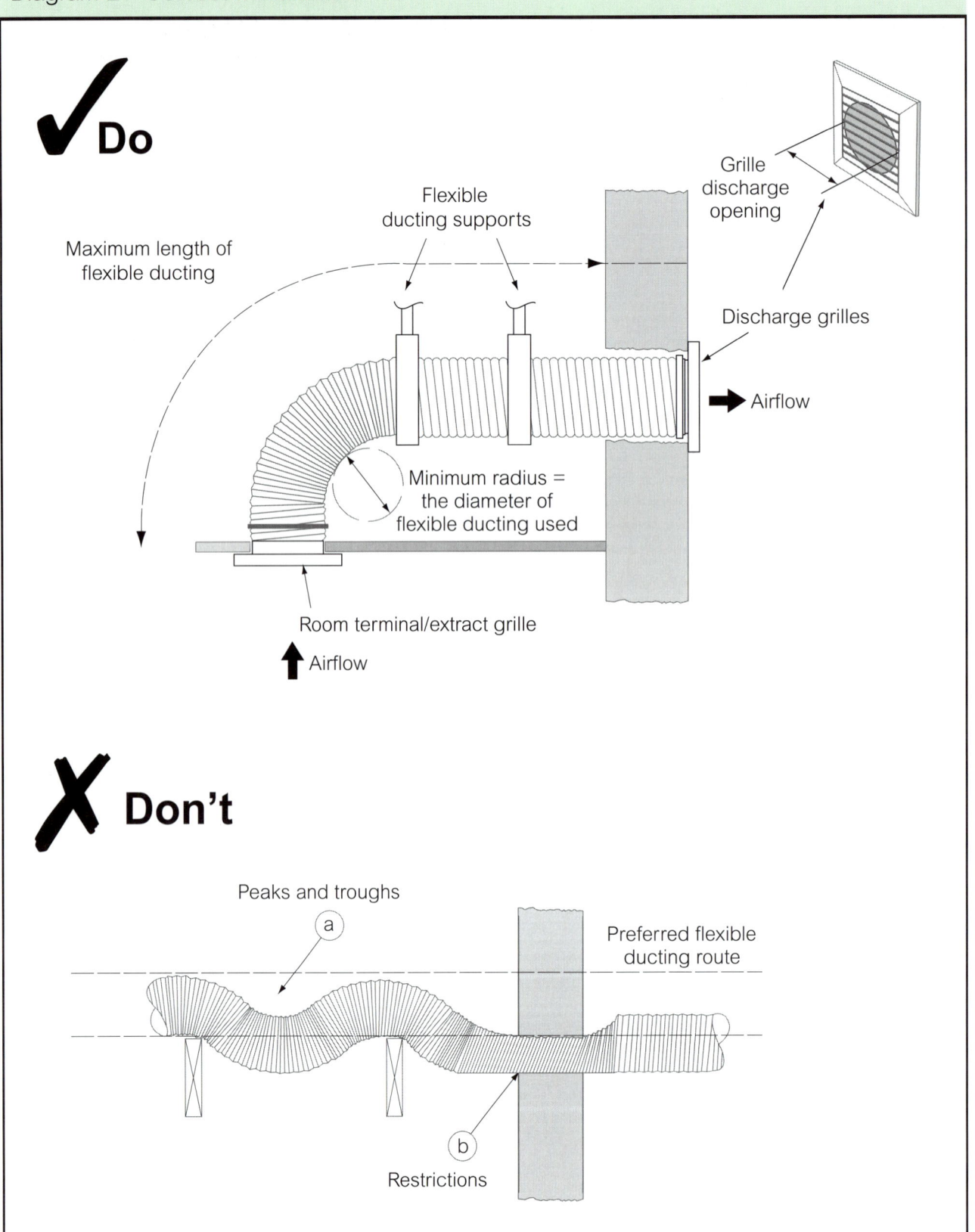

Appendix F: Minimising ingress of external pollution into buildings in urban areas

Typical urban pollutants that need to be considered include those covered by the UK Air Quality Strategy (DETR(2000)). These are:

- carbon monoxide, CO;

- nitrogen dioxide, NO_2;

- sulphur dioxide, SO_2;

- ozone, O_3;

- particles (PM_{10});

- benzene;

- 1,3-butadiene;

- lead.

Although nitrogen oxide, NO, is not included in the UK Air Quality Strategy, it is a normal constituent of combustion discharges and in many cases (for example, from gas-fired plant) the largest polluting emitter; therefore, it also needs to be taken into account.

Typical pollution emission sources that need to be considered include:

- road traffic, including traffic junctions and underground car parks;

- combustion plant (such as heating appliances) running on conventional fuels, most commonly natural gas;

- other combustion processes (for example, waste incineration, thermal oxidation abatement systems);

- discharges from industrial processes;

- fugitive (i.e. adventitious/not effectively controlled) discharges from industrial processes and other sources;

- building ventilation system exhaust discharges;

- construction and demolition sites which are source of particles and vapourous discharges.

In urban areas, buildings are exposed simultaneously to a large number of individual pollution sources from varying upwind distances (long range, intermediate range and short range) and heights and also over different timescales. The relationship between these and their proportionate contribution under different circumstances governs pollutant concentrations over the building shell and also internally.

Internal contamination of buildings from outdoor pollution sources therefore depends upon the pollutant sources, the physical characteristics of the building and its relation to its surroundings, the ventilation strategy employed and the location of the air intake. Whatever type of ventilation system is used, it is important to ensure that the intake air is not contaminated. This is especially important in air quality management areas where, by definition, pollution levels of at least one pollutant are already close to the air quality standards.

Simplified guidance on ventilation intake placement for minimising ingress of pollutants may be summarised, as in Table F1.

Table F1 **Guidance on ventilation intake placement for minimising ingress of pollutants**

Pollutant source	Recommendation
Local static sources: • Parking areas; • Welding areas; • Loading bays; • Adjacent building exhausts; • Stack discharges.	• Ventilation intakes need to be placed away from the direct impact of short-range pollution sources especially if the sources are within a few metres of the building. Some guidance is given in CIBSE TM21.
Urban traffic	• Air intakes for buildings positioned directly adjacent to urban roads should be as high as possible and away from the direct influence of the source so as to minimise the ingress of traffic pollutants. There will be exceptions to this simple guide and these risks may need to be assessed by modelling. In such case it is recommended that expert advice is sought. • For buildings located one or two streets away, the placement of intakes is less critical.
Building Features/Layout: • Courtyards; • Street canyons (i.e. a canyon formed in a street between two rows of tall buildings).	• Intakes should not be located in these spaces where there are air pollutant discharges. This included emission discharges from building ventilation system exhausts. • If air intakes are to be located in these spaces, they should be positioned as far as possible from the source in an open or well-ventilated area. In addition, steps should be taken to reduce the polluted source, e.g. parking and loading should be avoided as pollutants can accumulate in enclosed regions such as courtyards.
Multiple Sources	• Where there are large numbers of local sources, the combined effect of these around the façade of the building should be assessed. The façade experiencing the lowest concentration of the pollutants would be an obvious choice for locating ventilation intakes but this will require expert assistance such as numerical and wind tunnel modelling. In general, however, it is recommended that the air intakes be positioned as far from the source at a location where air is free to move around the intake.
Weather Factors	• In areas where predominant wind comes from opposing directions (e.g. a valley location) the air intakes and outlets should point in opposite directions. • In complex urban layouts, complex wind flows are likely to occur. In these cases, expert advice should be sought.

Control of ventilation intakes

For pollutant sources such as urban road traffic, whose concentration fluctuates with the time of day, reducing the flow of external air or closing ventilation intakes during peak periods of high external pollutant concentrations, for example during rush hours, for up to an hour may be an option.

Air intakes located on a less polluted side of the building may then be used for fresh air, or air may be fully re-circulated within the building. Alternatively, the building may be used as a 'fresh air' reservoir to supply air during these short periods. The use of atria as a source of 'fresh air' for this purpose may be an option.

However, care must be taken since, for example, reducing the inflow of external air will also reduce the outflow of internal air, resulting in a build-up of internally generated pollutants that need to be removed. Most modern buildings have low ceiling heights and therefore the concept of a substantial 'fresh air' reservoir available within the building may not apply. Further details of this principle with examples may be found in Liddament (2000).

Location of exhaust outlets

The location of exhausts is as important as the location of air intakes. These should be located such that re-entry to a building, or ingestion into other nearby buildings, is minimised (for both natural and mechanical intakes) and such that there is no adverse effect to the surrounding area. Guidance on outlet placement may be summarised as follows.

- Exhausts should be located downstream of intakes where there is a prevailing wind direction.

- Exhausts should not discharge into courtyards, enclosures or architectural screens as pollutants tend to build up in such spaces and do not disperse very readily.

- It is recommended that stacks should discharge vertically upwards and at high level to clear surrounding buildings and so that downwash does not occur.

- Where possible, pollutants from stacks should be grouped together and discharged vertically upwards. The increased volume will provide greater momentum and increased plume height. This is common practice where there are a number of fume cupboard discharges; greater plume height dispersion can be achieved by adding the general ventilation exhaust.

References

CIBSE (1999). CIBSE Technical Memorandum TM21. *Minimising Pollution at Air Intakes.* ISBN 0 90095 391 8

Liddament MW (2000) Chapter 13: Ventilation strategies. *Indoor Air Quality Handbook.* McGraw-Hill.